P[...]

SEX, LIES AN[...]
MORE SEX, LIES AND THE BALLOT BOX

'*Freakonomics* for political junkies. The perfect book
for anyone with even a passing interest in politics.'

'*Sex, Lies and the Ballot Box* is a revelation, a paperback with an
eye-catching title and essays by 51 political scientists ...
Superb and eminently quotable.'

'Smart, funny and illuminating in ways you could never dream of.'

'This book is such an utterly brilliant idea it is ridiculous that no one has
thought of it before. I cannot recommend it highly enough.'

'It's like Sgt Pepper but for political geeks.'

'A wonderful book of political well-I-nevers.'

'It does it with such aplomb that no political home's Christmas tree should
be without a copy neatly wrapped and waiting beneath it.'

'This knits academic research with accessible and thought-provoking questions. If you love elections you'll be hooked.'

'The political book that everybody's talking about.'

'*Sex, Lies and the Ballot Box* is as entertaining as it is thought-provoking.'

'Each chapter is a cruel and forensic exposé of the ill-informed clichés of political reporting. This book must be banned.'

'Finally, the one book you need before the election. This is a wonderfully eclectic collection of academic research translated into normal English.'

'A terrific book … Anyone interested in voting and elections would find it enlightening. If I could make it compulsory reading for people who follow my blog, I would…'

SEX, LIES AND POLITICS

THE SECRET INFLUENCES THAT DRIVE OUR POLITICAL CHOICES

EDITED BY
PHILIP COWLEY AND ROBERT FORD

Biteback Publishing

First published in Great Britain in 2019 by
Biteback Publishing Ltd
Westminster Tower
3 Albert Embankment
London SE1 7SP

ISBN 978-1-78590-506-3

10 9 8 7 6 5 4 3 2 1

A CIP catalogue record for this book is available from the British Library.

Set in Minion Pro and Trade Gothic

Printed and bound in Great Britain by
CPI Group (UK) Ltd, Croydon CR0 4YY

Contents

Foreword

A long, long time ago, so long ago that the governing party had a parliamentary majority and Labour were in power in England, Scotland, Wales *and* London, I used to be a political activist.

One thing that hasn't changed, though, was that the then leader of the Labour Party was not particularly popular and many people, including those who had voted for Labour for a long time, were very angry about a central issue of party policy and were threatening to vote Liberal Democrat. Or Conservative. Or UKIP. Or Esther Rantzen. Or, really, anyone who wasn't the Labour Party.

A good friend, who was about my age, used to go door-knocking with me. Door-knocking is a process whereby party members come to your door and ask a bunch of intrusive questions in the hope that you will vote for them in order to make them go away. Door-knocking was a pretty miserable experience and we had a game: to see if we could predict the voting intention of the people we were bothering based only on their front doors and windows.

Over time, we became quite good at it – the guessing, I mean – and had an increasingly elaborate series of indicators that could predict, to a reasonable degree of accuracy, how someone would vote based on just their door. Little did we realise at the time, but we had cracked the fundamentals of political science.

Of course, we couldn't *always* match the voter to the door, and political scientists aren't always right, either. Political scientists are the ones who told you that general election campaigns tend not to matter all that much, and that divided parties don't win elections. Well, OK, political journalists are the ones who told you that, but we only did it because a smart-looking person, or at least someone with the word 'professor' in their job title, told us that first.

So what's the point of this book? Why should we trust these people when they explain to us, as they will over the coming topics, why door-knocking really works, why polling is so hard to get right, and why ethnic minority Britons tend to vote Labour?

Well, it's partly of course that the alternative is listening to whatever half-baked reckons that any passing journalist can muster up from whoever happens to be willing to talk to us in the middle of the day. Just as we couldn't *always* get the door right, this is a book that will entertain you, inform you and will, at least, mostly be right.

Equally importantly, just as years and years after I let my membership lapse and even longer since I last knocked on a door, I still smile whenever I see a messy window box or a mattress on the front lawn, this is a book that will change how you think about politics. Even if sometimes the man with a mattress in his garden *is* voting for David Cameron after all.

Stephen Bush

Introduction

Philip Cowley and Robert Ford

Elections are important. But that isn't the only reason some people spend their lives studying them.

Elections are also, at least some of the time, interesting, fun, shocking and exciting. Yet that's not why you should study them either.

Elections are always revealing. Those willing to dig into the detail of elections and voting will find human nature, in all its dizzying variety, contained within. That is why they are worth studying.

This is a book about elections not as a means of choosing governments but as a means to learn about the human condition, and about what makes us tick. 'If we would learn what the human race really is at bottom', claimed Mark Twain, 'we need only observe it at election time' – and the only thing that has changed since Twain wrote that in 1885 is that the more we learn about elections, the more we realise how accurate he was.

Like all things involving human beings, the reality of elections is often a long way from the myth – and it isn't always uplifting. It can, for example, be a bit depressing to learn that candidates with surnames that begin with a letter that comes early on in the alphabet have an advantage over those lower down. Or that better-looking candidates will out-perform the ugly ones. Or that both Leave and Remain voters think Postman Pat is one of their own. All this is true, and is discussed in what follows.

But at the same time it is uplifting to discover that, for all the criticism voters can get (and give), they haven't completely lost faith in politics despite all its flaws; they respond fairly coherently to what governments do, even if they don't know the details; most of them will get off the couch and vote if only someone asks them nicely; and they really do try their best, most of the time, to make sense of a difficult and confusing political world and vote in accordance with what they value most.

The genesis of this book lies in two earlier volumes, *Sex, Lies and the Ballot Box* and its imaginatively named follow-up, *More Sex, Lies and the Ballot Box*. Both books were well received and sold well enough. (By this we mean they sold well for books on how people vote, not that J. K. Rowling became unduly concerned for her sales by the appearance of a rival.) This volume contains a combination of chapters from the two earlier books – revised, where appropriate – along with many entirely new chapters, largely, but not exclusively, dealing with Brexit. Indeed, so much has changed since the first book came out in 2014 that even some of the revised chapters have been so thoroughly altered that they are essentially new. Whatever one's views on Brexit, both the referendum and events since have been full of what educators call 'teachable moments', things that perfectly illustrate how people, on all sides, are not quite as rational or all-knowing as they like to think they are.

The chapters are written by members of the Political Studies

Association's specialist group on Elections, Public Opinion and Parties, known as EPOP, which has been running for over twenty years and is one of the PSA's most active groups. The book is written by people who love elections so much that the electoral cycle is part of the natural rhythm of their lives.* We know that many of our readers will be similarly enthused, but there is also another goal, and another audience, for the book: to try to reach people who had perhaps not realised how interesting elections and voting can be.

The study of voting – psephology, as it is known – draws on a range of materials, from electoral results to focus groups with voters to opinion polling. The chapters that follow make use of all of these types of sources. Britain, in particular, is lucky in the breadth and depth of data available to researchers seeking to understand the public mood.

Yet recent years have provided plenty of fodder for polling sceptics. Neither of us can say anything about polls on social media these days without some smart alec popping up to announce that 'you can't trust polls any more', as a result of Trump or Brexit or Corbyn (or whatever is their obsession). The first problem with this argument is that it often isn't true. American pollsters, for example, correctly predicted a popular vote win for Hillary Clinton (it's not their fault the voters lived in the wrong places) and, as one of the chapters in this book makes clear, polls in recent elections across the globe have performed as well as they ever have, if not better.

---

* One of this volume's editors uses the date of Boris Johnson's first election victory to help him remember his wedding anniversary – something even the other editor thinks is, frankly, a little bit sad.

Polls are sometimes wrong, but they are always uncertain, and the bigger problem with polling is that this uncertainty gets lost in the stories people build from them. The idea that Trump couldn't win or that Brexit was impossible was a narrative crafted by pundits and campaigners – the polls were never so certain. We know polls will go wrong sometimes, but we also know that people are very prone to leap to strong conclusions based on limited evidence. Some argue that the errors in the polls are so frequent, or our ability to judge them properly so limited, that they do more harm than good to our election campaigns, or even to our broader political conversation. Perhaps, such critics say, it is time to do away with the distraction of unreliable polls altogether. We think the opposite; with so much up in the air, it is more important than ever to keep ourselves grounded with the best evidence about the public mood that we can gather. Polls and analysts get things wrong sometimes. But get rid of them and the vacuum will only be filled with bad punditry and biased speculation, which will get more things more wrong, more often. Ignorance, as Barack Obama once said, is never a virtue; it's just not knowing stuff.

That said, no one who does it seriously thinks that measuring public opinion is without difficulties. As many of the chapters in this book demonstrate, the public can give different responses to almost identical questions; they have inconsistent attitudes; voters can support or oppose policies that do not exist; voters often think they voted when they didn't (and think they didn't when they did). In *Yes, Minister*, there is an exchange between the Permanent Secretary Sir Humphrey Appleby and the more junior Bernard Woolley after Bernard presents some unwelcome opinion poll data and is told to go away and do another poll producing the opposite response. Bernard protests that the public can't be both for and against something. Sir Humphrey's response: 'Of course they can, Bernard.' And Sir Humphrey was right. But polling is still better than the alternative – which is to make it up or to assume that you or your friends have some profound insight into the general population (spoiler alert: you don't). The answer to poor polling is not no polling but better polling, along with a better understanding of what the polls can (and can't) tell us.

Here are fourteen rules to help understand polls and polling:

1. *Be sceptical about genuine polls but ignore the voodoo ones entirely.* The first question to ask is simple: is this a genuine poll? Is it carried out by a reputable company, which has attempted to ensure that the people taking part are broadly representative of the public? Even good companies get things wrong occasionally, so some scepticism is always justified, and there are legitimate debates over the best way to tap into the public mood. But it's fairly easy to spot the ones that aren't pukka. Is it a self-selecting poll on a newspaper website or a phone-in poll on TV? Is it someone using Twitter to push for a 'big sample'? The views of 10,000 activists on Twitter are no more informative or representative than the views of ten of your mates around a pub table (that is: not informative at all). If it's any of these so-called voodoo polls, don't waste your time being sceptical. Just ignore it altogether.

2. *If a poll looks especially unusual or interesting, it is probably wrong.* This is known as 'Twyman's Law' after Tony Twyman, a media research analyst. Eye-catching polling results are often the product of some blunder by the pollster, such

as a poorly designed question, or due to the vagaries of sampling. Plus, chance alone will throw up the occasional outlier with eye-catching results from time to time. This wouldn't be much of a problem, except…

3. *If a poll looks unusual or interesting, it will get more headlines.* 'Poll shows same as the poll we did last week' isn't a headline. 'Poll shows dramatic and unexpected shift' is a headline. As a result, what people read about polling tends to be skewed towards the errors and outliers, and towards change over stability (even when the change is within the margin of error). The blame for this doesn't rest solely with journalists or editors; anyone following polls on social media can see it is the outliers that rack up the likes and retweets. We are all suckers for surprises.

4. *Polls aren't as precise as people sometimes pretend.* Given all this, it is worth remembering that even an absolutely kosher poll has the potential for error of around +/- 3 percentage points on any single finding. (On a combination of findings, such as the lead of one party over another, the potential random error is even larger.) It is therefore always better to focus on trends over time – is the lead getting larger or smaller? – than obsessing over any one poll finding. And be especially cautious about analysing parts of any poll – what are called the cross-breaks – such as the figures just for men, or those in London, or working-class people. Here, the numbers involved will be smaller and the random error larger still.

5. *The public isn't stupid, they're just not all that interested.* Most people don't pay attention to politics most of the time. This is hard for those whose job it is to follow politics 24/7 to

understand or take into account, and it can lead to problems. Sometimes people are asked questions in polls which assume a level of knowledge about politicians or policies that most people simply don't have. Even then, most voters will gamely try their best using whatever hints are provided in the question to guide them on unfamiliar terrain. Ambitious campaigners can exploit this tendency to pump up support for an obscure politician or proposal, by linking them to something better known or popular. But don't underestimate the public – they can pick up the drift of developments even if they seem to know nothing about the detail. As a result…

6. *How you ask the question matters.* Everyone involved in polling knows that question wording matters – and so reputable companies take real pains over it. There is a good reason for this: most people know what they think in broad-brush terms but know little about detailed or obscure issues, so they will look for hints in the question to help them make sense of it. As a result, even small changes in how a question is asked can produce a big shift in responses, if the change alters what voters think the question means (as discussed in Chapter 1). This effect also highlights that what the question writers think their question is about is often very different from what a typical voter thinks it is about.

7. *People see the world through partisan lenses.* Most of us are not neutral. We have a team we cheer for and a team we oppose. When new information appears, these allegiances skew how we understand it. Many of the chapters below show how partisan filters affect the way people respond to polling questions (even when they apply to fictional characters, marital infidelity

or cats). You can also watch this process unfold in real time on social media whenever a poll is published – partisans will sing the merits of strong polls for their party, which they are eager to share, while criticising or ignoring less-flattering polling. Reverse the poll results, and the critics and cheerleaders switch sides.

8. *People don't always tell the truth.* People routinely claim to be much better citizens than they are – the numbers claiming they watch political coverage regularly, or who will turn out to vote, are far above the true figures revealed by TV ratings and election tallies. People are also so unwilling to admit their ignorance that most will happily attempt to answer meaningless or illogical questions. These fibs are still revealing, though – because they show how people want to be thought of as good citizens and don't like admitting ignorance.

9. *People aren't good at predicting (or remembering) what influences them.* If you ask people, 'Would x influence your vote?', they often say 'Yes'. But if people were that easily influenced, elections would be much more volatile and less predictable than they are. People simply aren't very good at understanding their own decision processes and systematically overestimate the importance of whatever notion a pollster puts in front of them. For exactly this reason, 'Would x influence your vote?' questions are very popular with campaign groups, who will tout the answers as evidence of the burning importance of their pet issue.

10. *Individuals are unique, but crowds are more predictable.* Everyone's heard about a relative who lived to a ripe old age despite

cheerfully inhaling sixty a day. Few people think that means smoking isn't harmful for your health. The elderly relative is just an outlier. People understand this at one level: they know that the same forces impact on everyone exposed to them, moving them all together. But everyone also thinks they are the exception to the rule: 'Moving in crowds is what other people do; I take my own path.' Both views are right. Studying public opinion is often like watching pebbles on a beach – every pebble looks unique, starts in a unique place, and moves in a unique way. But all the pebbles are pushed by the same wave, and they tend to move in the same general direction.

11. *Crowds may be more predictable, but they're not uniform.* At any election or referendum, it is common to hear commentators declare that that 'the people' think something or other. This is always nonsense, because 'the people' never think just one thing. The only certainty in life is that, even if many, or most, people think x, there are still plenty of people who think y, along with some who think both x and y, some who don't know, some who won't say, some who think they think x but really think y, some who say they think y but go and vote for x anyway, and so on.

12. *Accusations of pollster bias usually say more about the accuser than the pollster.* Political polling is a high-stakes public relations exercise for pollsters; it is their opportunity to demonstrate how good they are at gauging public opinion. They spend a lot of time and effort trying to be as accurate and unbiased as possible. Those who attack pollsters as biased

are usually the most biased of all – partisans who do not have any incentive to be accurate and every incentive to attack the bearers of bad news about their team.

13. *Public opinion is part of politics, but it is not the same as politics.* A well-conducted poll can tell you what people are thinking; it does not tell politicians what to do. Public opinion can change, not least because politicians can try to change it. When Bob Hawke, then Prime Minister of Australia, was told that he needed to be careful how he handled a racially sensitive issue, because some of his supporters held racist attitudes, he replied: 'Then tell me what I need to say to turn them around.' Too much analysis of polling presents it as the end-product of politics rather than just part of the process.

14. *Most people think everything in politics has an obvious explanation.* They are wrong, as the rest of this book will demonstrate.

Like its predecessors, this book isn't meant to be an introductory textbook. This volume offers an eclectic series of sketches, each introducing an aspect of elections and political behaviour. Each of the chapters offers a 1,000-word essay. These are not monographs, and most of them summarise years, in some cases decades, of research. Each chapter ends with a short account of further reading, and there is a detailed bibliography in case any of the subject matter stirs you to dig deeper. We make no claim for comprehensiveness, but between them the following fifty chapters incorporate: polling, ignorance, political geography, targeting, gender, sex, race, racism, Scotland, partisanship, Wales, young people, trust, turnout, apathy, alienation, death, volatility, religion, issue ownership and salience, Northern Ireland, manifestos, candidates, class and Brexit. And then more sex.

As with the two earlier books, our colleagues were enthusiastic about the book and a pleasure to work with. Editing a book like this was not always straightforward, but they have made it easier by always (well, almost always) responding to our often detailed and insistent editorial requests swiftly and in good spirit. We are also grateful to all the staff at Biteback for their support. We think the end result is worth it. We hope you do too.

List of contributors

NICHOLAS ALLEN is Reader in Politics at Royal Holloway, University of London.

BEN ANSELL is Professor of Comparative Democratic Institutions at the University of Oxford.

ROGER AWAN-SCULLY is Professor of Political Science and Head of Politics and International Relations at Cardiff University.

NEEMA BEGUM is Research Associate in the Centre on the Dynamics of Ethnicity at the University of Manchester.

GALINA BORISYUK is Chief Data Scientist at BMG Research.

ROSIE CAMPBELL is Director of the Global Institute for Women's Leadership and Professor of Politics at King's College London.

PHILIP COWLEY is Professor of Politics at Queen Mary University of London.

JOHN CURTICE is Professor of Politics at Strathclyde.

DAVID CUTTS is Professor of Political Science at the University of Birmingham.

JAMES DENNISON is Research Fellow at the European University Institute.

DAVID DENVER is Emeritus Professor of Politics at Lancaster University.

DANNY DORLING is Halford Mackinder Professor of Geography at the University of Oxford.

GEOFFREY EVANS is Professor in the Sociology of Politics and Official Fellow of Nuffield College at the University of Oxford.

JOCELYN EVANS is Professor of Politics at the University of Leeds.

STEPHEN FISHER is Associate Professor in Political Sociology at the University of Oxford and a Fellow of Trinity College.

ROBERT FORD is Professor of Political Science at the University of Manchester.

STUART FOX is Lecturer in British Politics at Brunel University London.

JANE GREEN is Professor of Political Science and British Politics at Nuffield College, Oxford.

CHRIS HANRETTY is Professor of Politics at Royal Holloway, University of London.

ANTHONY HEATH is Emeritus Professor of Sociology at the University of Oxford and the University of Manchester and Emeritus Fellow of Nuffield College, Oxford, where he is Director of the Centre for Social Investigation.

OLIVER HEATH is Professor in Politics at Royal Holloway, University of London.

JENNIFER VAN HEERDE-HUDSON is Professor in Political Behaviour at University College London.

AILSA HENDERSON is Professor of Political Science at the University of Edinburgh.

WILL JENNINGS is Professor of Political Science and Public Policy at the University of Southampton.

ROB JOHNS is Professor in Politics at the University of Essex.

REBECCA MCKEE is Research Fellow at the Constitution Unit at University College London.

NICOLE MARTIN is Lecturer in Politics at the University of Manchester.

JONATHAN MELLON is Hallsworth Research Fellow at the University of Manchester.

CAITLIN MILAZZO is Associate Professor in Politics at the University of Nottingham.

JAMES MORRIS is Senior Director at Edelman.

MARK PACK is Associate Director at communications agency Teneo.

CHARLES PATTIE is Professor of Politics at the University of Sheffield.

CHRISTOPHER PROSSER is Presidential Fellow at the University of Manchester.

KINGSLEY PURDAM is Senior Lecturer at the University of Manchester.

ALAN RENWICK is Associate Professor in British Politics and Deputy Director of the Constitution Unit at University College London.

LINDSAY RICHARDS is Lecturer in Sociology at the University of Oxford and an associate member of the Centre for Social Investigation, Nuffield College.

ELINE DE ROOIJ is Associate Professor in Political Science at Simon Fraser University.

ROSALIND SHORROCKS is Lecturer in Politics at the University of Manchester.

MARIA SOBOLEWSKA is Professor of Political Science at the University of Manchester.

PATRICK STURGIS is Professor of Quantitative Social Science at the London School of Economics and Political Science.

PAULA SURRIDGE is Senior Lecturer at the University of Bristol.

JAMES TILLEY is Professor of Politics at the University of Oxford and a Fellow of Jesus College.

JON TONGE is Professor of Politics at the University of Liverpool.

JOE TWYMAN is co-founder of Deltapoll.

MARKUS WAGNER is Professor for Quantitative Methods in Political Science at the University of Vienna.

ANTHONY WELLS is Director of Political and Social Research at YouGov and writes the independent UKPollingReport.co.uk blog.

PAUL WHITELEY is Professor of Politics at the University of Essex.

NICOLA WILDASH is Senior Analyst for Quantitative Research at Sport England.

BERNADETA WILK is Chief Data Officer at Populus.

CHRISTOPHER WLEZIEN is Hogg Professor of Government at the University of Texas at Austin.

'A most wretched custom, assuredly, is our electioneering and scrambling for office.'

– CICERO, 44BC

'People never lie so much as after a hunt, during a war or before an election.'

– ATTRIBUTED TO OTTO VON BISMARCK

'At any given moment, public opinion is a chaos of superstition, misinformation, and prejudice.'

– GORE VIDAL

'The people have spoken, the bastards.'

– DICK TUCK, AFTER LOSING A CALIFORNIA STATE SENATE RACE IN 1966

CHAPTER 1

Slippery polls: why public opinion is so difficult to measure

Rob Johns

I magine a fantasy world in which the British government wanted only to follow public opinion. With no agenda of its own, the Cabinet would sit down weekly to plan how to translate the latest polls directly into public policy. This government would find life very difficult; it would be prone to frequent U-turns and would rapidly become frustrated with its public masters. The problem is the slippery nature of opinion polls. Questions asked about the same issue on the same day can often carry different, even directly contradictory, messages about public preferences.

One common explanation for this, the case of deliberately leading questions, can be swiftly dismissed. Everyone knows that a question along the lines of 'Do you support Policy X or do you oppose this ill-conceived and dangerous idea?' will reduce support for Policy X, and the major pollsters refuse to field such obviously biased questions. Such blatant bias is now largely confined to opt-in polls on the websites of tabloid newspapers.

The real difficulty for pollsters and those poring over their results is that even ostensibly neutral questions can be strikingly inconsistent. Consider one of the earliest question-wording experiments, a 1940 survey in which American respondents were randomly chosen to receive one of two questions about free speech. The results are in the table, which also shows what happened when the experiment was re-run three decades later. Americans in 1940 were a lot more comfortable in 'not allowing' (75 per cent) than in 'forbidding' (54 per cent) speeches against democracy. By 1974, the results were more befitting of the Land of the Free but the big difference between question wordings remained. The nature of that difference makes sense – forbidding something sounds harsher than merely not allowing it – but its scale is troubling. Are public preferences on issues as fundamental as free speech really so weak as to be dramatically shifted by a change in emphasis?

THE FORBID/ALLOW ASYMMETRY IN QUESTION-WORDING

	ALLOW/NOT FORBID (%)	NOT ALLOW/FORBID (%)
1940 EXPERIMENT		
Group A: Do you think the US should allow public speeches against democracy?	25	75
Group B: Do you think the US should forbid public speeches against democracy?	46	54
1974 EXPERIMENT		
Group A: Allow public speeches against democracy?	52	48
Group B: Forbid public speeches against democracy?	71	21

To answer that question, it is useful to sketch Paul (or Paula), the typical survey respondent. Politics is low on his agenda and, as a result, many of the questions asked by pollsters are on issues to which Paul has given little previous thought. As American researcher Philip Converse concluded, many people simply 'do not have meaningful beliefs, even on issues that have formed the basis for intense political controversy among elites for substantial periods of time'. But Paul is an obliging type and can't help feeling that, if a pollster is asking him about an issue, he really ought to have a view on it. So he will avoid saying, 'Don't know' and oblige with an answer. (As Chapter 3 shows, respondents are often happy to answer even when pollsters ask about fictional policies.)

How, then, does Paul answer these questions? Not purely at random because, even with unfamiliar issues, there are links to more familiar and deeply held attitudes and values. For example, if Paul were asked whether he would support restrictions on UK arms sales to Saudi Arabia, he might say 'yes' on the grounds that fewer weapons in circulation is generally a good thing or 'no' on the grounds that British exports support British jobs. None of this requires him even to know where Saudi Arabia is on the map. However, the other thing about Paul is that he is a little lazy, at least in cognitive terms. Rather than addressing the question from all relevant angles, balancing conflicting considerations to reach a judgement, he is prone to answer on the basis of whatever comes immediately to mind. If the previous night's news contained graphic images of suffering in a conflict zone, Paul will probably support restricting arms sales; if instead there was a story about manufacturing job losses, he is likely to oppose it.

This 'top-of-the-head' nature of survey answers is what gives the question wording such power. Any small cue or steer in the question is, by definition, at the top of people's heads when answering.

Attributions are one common cue. In the early 2000s the Conservative Party found that many of its new ideas were quite popular in opinion polls – unless the poll mentioned that they were Conservative policies, in which case that popularity ebbed. If the proposal to restrict arms sales were attributed to Labour or to Jeremy Corbyn in particular, respondents might just respond according to their partisan or personal sympathies (and see Chapters 16 and 43 for how this applies even to cats and fictional characters).

Now imagine that the question asked about 'arms sales to the authoritarian regime in Saudi Arabia'. Paul and many others would be more supportive of restrictions. This doesn't mean that the lack of democracy in Saudi is *really* a decisive factor in public judgements outside the context of the survey; it means that the question elbows other considerations out of respondents' minds. Or suppose that the arms sales question itself was studiedly neutral but that it was preceded by a series of questions about instability and conflict around the world. The effect would be much the same.

Another common steer comes in the sadly ubiquitous questions based on declarative statements. For example, another survey experiment found majority agreement (60 per cent) with the statement 'Individuals are more to blame than social conditions for crime in this country'. But the survey also found almost the same level of agreement (57 per cent) with the exact opposite statement: 'Social conditions are more to blame than individuals for crime in this country'. This is because the statements used in the question have persuasive power in themselves. It is easier for unsure (and lazy) respondents to agree with the assertion than consider the alternatives. No wonder there was opposition to the Scottish government's original proposal for the 2014 referendum question: 'Do you agree that Scotland should be an independent country?'

Lastly, consider the choice between open and closed questions. Polls often ask, 'What do you think is the most important problem facing Britain today?' In the 'closed' version, where respondents choose from a list, crime is a popular choice. Yet in an 'open' version, where respondents have to name an issue unprompted, crime is much less often mentioned. Maybe a list helps to remind people of their genuine concerns, but then is crime *that* troubling to someone who can't remember it unaided?

All of this illustrates the persistent difficulty for our fantasy government. Even the most discerning consumer of opinion polls, who well understands why two surveys deliver different results, might still struggle to say which better reflects what the public really thinks. Some have even drawn the radical conclusion that 'true' attitudes simply don't exist. This seems overstated, however. For one thing, people do have strong views on the big issues that they care about. It is when pollsters ask about more remote topics that opinions look so fickle. Second, even when respondents appear malleable, this is not simply swaying in the breeze; it is because something in the question leads them to consider the issue in a different way.

Public opinion thus has at least some anchoring in people's most deeply held beliefs and values. Perhaps a preferable conclusion is that the truths are out there – but that there are many of them and they may be quite different. This, of course, provides exactly the leeway that real governments are after.

FURTHER READING

The quotation from Philip Converse is taken from his 1964 essay on 'The nature of belief systems in mass publics'. A 'one-stop shop' for question-wording effects is the book *Questions and Answers in Attitude Surveys* by Howard Schuman and Stanley Presser (Sage, 1996). For informed commentary on UK opinion polling, with frequent reminders of the pitfalls discussed in this chapter, consult the blogs UK Polling Report and Number Cruncher Politics.

—CHAPTER 2—

Not getting worse: polling accuracy

Christopher Wlezien

Early in the morning on 8 May 2015, it became clear that the UK polling industry had a problem. Throughout the campaign the polls indicated that the Conservatives and Labour were neck-and-neck and a hung parliament was highly probable. When the votes were counted, however, David Cameron's Conservatives had achieved their first majority in over twenty years, based on a sizeable seven-point victory over Labour in the national vote. The official inquiry into the 2015 pre-election polls found that they had suffered from unrepresentative samples. Polls in the UK missed again – perhaps more famously – in the Brexit referendum of 2016, with those conducted on the eve of the vote pointing to a slim win for Remain.

The surprise victory of Donald Trump in the US presidential election in 2016 similarly fuelled talk of a crisis in the polling industry. While pollsters in fact were quite close to the national result, they put the votes in the wrong places. Polls were badly off in a few key swing states in the Midwest, underestimating turn-out of white non-college voters, a key demographic that delivered

Trump the states of Pennsylvania, Michigan and Wisconsin, and the White House. This also led to methodological soul-searching among pollsters, as well as repeated claims that polls could no longer be trusted.

Yet there is little evidence that polls are becoming more inaccurate. Rather than one-off cases, consider the accuracy of polls in over 300 general elections in forty-five countries since the 1940s. To measure accuracy, let's use the 'absolute error' as our measure of polling accuracy; that is, the absolute difference between the polls and the election result. If the polls put a party or candidate at 45 per cent and they receive 47 per cent of the actual vote, this would be an absolute error of 2 points. This measure can be useful for showing how polls line up with voters' eventual choices over the course of the election. About 200 days out from election day, the average absolute difference between the polls and the subsequent election result is around 4 percentage points. Fifty days out, this difference declines to about 3 percentage points, while on the eve of election day it is close to 2 points. As the election gets nearer, polls are increasingly informative about voters' preferences, as one would expect.

To test whether polling accuracy has declined across years, you need to look at the average absolute error of polls in the final week of the election campaign. This is shown in the figure, where the black circle indicates the average error across all parties and candidates in a given year, and the grey line indicates the trend. These results reveal no significant upward trend in polling errors that popular accounts would suggest. The mean polling error across all elections in the entire period from 1942 to 2017 is 2.1 per cent. Since the 2000s the polling error has, if anything, been slightly lower than the historical average – 2.0 per cent. There is no long-term upward trend in polling error, and indeed if we consider just those countries where pollsters have been active since the 1970s it appears that polling errors are actually declining.

ABSOLUTE VOTE–POLL ERRORS, 1942–2017

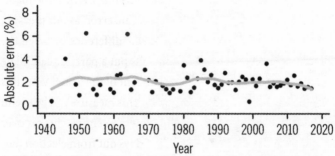

Source: Jennings & Wlezien (2018). The light grey line tracks the average error in political polls in the last week of the campaign over seventy-five years.

Some features of electoral systems and political parties can make it more or less difficult for pollsters to reliably measure voters' intentions. On average, polling errors are higher in presidential elections, lower in PR systems and greater for larger parties, those receiving more than 20 per cent of the vote. In PR systems, voting behaviour seems more predictable due to the central role of partisan loyalties in vote choice. In presidential elections, voters' preferences are less structured due to greater uncertainty about the candidates and their platforms. For larger parties, simple (mathematical) proportionality operates – that is, the larger the party, the greater the absolute errors – but sampling error does too, as it increases with party size, at least up to a 50 per cent vote share.

Yet there is a paradox here: although polling accuracy is improving, many people seem to believe the polls are getting worse. One possible explanation is that the public and media suffer from negativity bias – noticing and long remembering the times that polls went wrong, and ignoring or quickly forgetting those elections when they perform well. People's assessments of the polls may also be based more on whether they get the story right, rather than how accurate they are in statistical terms. The polls in the second round of the 2017 French presidential election were substantially off, yet this prompted little discussion since the result was the one polling had led people to expect – a comfortable Macron victory. One development that may be creating unrealistic expectations of polling (and error) is its role as an ingredient in the now popular business of political forecasting.

One recent study suggests that probabilistic forecasts lead people to be over-confident about the certainty of the election result, just because people do not fully understand probabilities. This serves to increase the degree of surprise when the declared election result is different to the one forecasts said was most likely.

That the accuracy of polling has remained so stable over three-quarters of a century is noteworthy when we consider the significant technological and methodological changes that have transpired in the industry, from face-to-face sampling to telephone polling to online surveys, and despite declining response rates from the public, and many changes in how pollsters adjust their samples.

FURTHER READING

The official reports into polls for the UK 2015 general election (Sturgis et al.'s 'Report of the Inquiry into the 2015 British general election opinion polls') and the US 2016 presidential election (Courtney Kennedy et al.'s 'An Evaluation of 2016 Election Polls in the United States, *Public Opinion Quarterly*, 2018) highlight many of the methodological challenges facing pollsters today. The cross-national study of polling accuracy is detailed in Will Jennings and Christopher Wlezien's 'Election Polling Errors Across Time and Space' (*Nature Human Behaviour*, 2018). For the effects of probabilistic forecasts on perceptions of electoral competitiveness and turnout see Sean Westwood et al.'s 'Projecting Confidence: How the Probabilistic Horse Race Confuses and Demobilizes the Public'.

CHAPTER 3

Why one in ten Britons support the Monetary Control Bill (even though it doesn't exist): public opinion and nonattitudes

Patrick Sturgis

In nearly every survey there are some people who tell pollsters that they do not have an opinion on an issue. But the number willing to volunteer ignorance in this way often appears smaller than it should be, given that many people know and care very little about politics. How, then, do voters decide where they stand on unfamiliar areas of public policy when asked about them in polls?

As noted in Chapter 1, a radical answer to this question was proposed in the '60s by American political scientist Philip Converse. Converse suggested that, on many issues, a substantial minority of the public has no opinion at all. Rather, they express what he referred to as 'nonattitudes'. A nonattitude is an answer to an opinion question which has no underlying cognitive or emotional basis; people select from the available response options more or less at random, as if 'mentally flipping a coin'.

If such 'nonattitudes' are widespread, the implications for democratic politics, as well as for the polling industry, would be problematic.

It is difficult to assess how big a problem nonattitudes really are, however, because from their outwardly observable characteristics at least, attitudes and nonattitudes are identical. An expedient solution to the problem of identifying the prevalence of nonattitudes is to ask people their opinions on issues which sound real but do not actually exist. People who are willing to provide an opinion on a plausible-sounding but fictitious policy issue are, we may assume, also likely to offer similarly empty opinions on real issues which they know little or nothing about.

The idea of identifying nonattitudes in this way stretches back at least as far as the '40s, when pollster Sam Gill speculated that up to 70 per cent of Americans would provide an opinion on the (non-existent) Metallic Metals Act. However, serious academic consideration of public opinion about fictitious issues did not start until the '80s, when George Bishop and colleagues at the University of Cincinnati found that a third of Americans either favoured or opposed the fictitious Public Affairs Act. Bishop found that this figure dropped substantially when respondents were offered an explicit 'Don't know' option. However, 10 per cent of respondents still selected a substantive answer, even when given a clear opportunity to express their lack of familiarity. Similar findings were reported in the US at around the same time by Howard Schuman and Stanley Presser, who also found that a third of respondents to their survey expressed positions on issues which, though real, were so obscure that few ordinary citizens would ever have heard of them.

And, despite the British generally considering themselves to be intellectually superior to their American cousins, recent research found significant proportions of the British public were also willing to express views on fictitious policy issues. It isn't possible to make direct comparisons between the British and the American research, because the questions posed and response alternatives offered were rather different. However, the British study found that 15 per cent of the British public either supported or opposed the non-existent 'Monetary Control Bill', while 11 per cent expressed a position on the equally fictitious 'Agricultural Trade Bill'.

So, non-trivial numbers of citizens are willing to offer opinions on issues which do not exist. Are they really selecting a response option at random, as Converse suggested? Probably not. Research has shown that responses to these fictitious issues are related to existing partisan tendencies. For example, in the British research, Conservative supporters were twice as likely to express an opinion on the Agricultural Trade Bill, compared to people who did not identify with a political party. This suggests that respondents do not choose their answers to fictitious issues at random but, rather, seek to determine what the issue is about and how it relates to their political predispositions, through clues in the wording of the question. In this instance, 'agricultural trade' sounds like legislation promoting free trade, so Conservative supporters interpret it as something which they should, on the face of it at least, favour.

Another sign that these opinions are not just random expressions of ignorance comes from the somewhat counter-intuitive finding that people who reported being very interested in politics

were more likely (23 per cent) to provide an opinion on the fictitious bills than those who expressed no interest at all (11 per cent).
The British research also found that men were 50 per cent more
likely to express a view on the Agricultural Trade Bill than women.
So, responding to fictitious issues seems to result, at least in part,
from considering yourself to be the sort of person who *should*
have a view on matters of public interest. Many voters know little or nothing about more obscure parts of the political agenda,
but voters who have already proclaimed their general interest in
politics may be too embarrassed to admit ignorance when subsequently asked their position on specific issues.

Despite the seemingly flippant nature of the exercise, then,
research on fictitious issues tells us at least two interesting things
about how people respond to questions relating to real policy
issues in polls. First, people do not choose a response option at
random from the tops of their heads but are, instead, actively seeking to understand what the question is about. They then provide
their best guess at what their position is, based on their political
orientation and the limited information available to them about
the issue. This helps explain why the 'framing' of a survey question can matter so much to the shape of public opinion elicited;
the exact terms used to describe an issue can strongly affect how
voters understand what it is about and, therefore, how they feel
about it. Be that as it may, fictitious issues research also tells us
that a great many answers to genuine policy questions in surveys are likely to be based on little more than informed guessing,
following a brief moment of reflection. This may not come as a
surprise to many observers of contemporary politics. However, it
serves as a cautionary reminder to all those who proffer opinion

poll evidence in order to show they have public backing for a particular policy position; the mandate they are citing is probably weaker than it appears.

FURTHER READING

Bishop's study on the US is 'Pseudo-Opinions on Public Affairs' by George Bishop et al. (*Public Opinion Quarterly*, 1980). The British study can be found in Patrick Sturgis and Patten Smith 'Fictitious Issues Revisited: Political Interest, Knowledge and the Generation of Nonattitudes' (*Political Studies*, 2010). Other relevant studies are Howard Schuman and Stanley Presser's 'Public Opinion and Public Ignorance: The Fine Line between Attitudes and Nonattitudes' (*American Journal of Sociology*, 1980) and George Bishop's *The Illusion of Public Opinion: Fact and Artifact in American Public Opinion Polls* (Rowman & Littlefield, 2005).

—CHAPTER 4—

When people don't know what they are going to do: meaningless polling questions

Anthony Wells

Every scandal and surprise in politics inevitably prompts a debate over what it means for the parties' poll standings. The most sensible (but dull) way of testing this is to compare voting intentions before and after the event to see if there has been any effect. The alternative approach is to ask people directly if the event has changed how they will vote. In a perfect world these two approaches would show the same result. In practice they often don't.

In *The Independent* in January 2013 a ComRes poll found 30 per cent of people agreeing they were more likely to vote Conservative because David Cameron had promised to hold a referendum on Europe. In the month leading up to Cameron's pledge, the average level of Conservative support in the polls was 31 per cent. In the month following, the average was still 31 per cent. Despite the poll, the pledge had made no difference. Why would so many people *claim* that the issue had the power to change their minds, when it clearly did not?

One reason is that such questions take an issue out of context and give it false prominence. If you only ask questions about, say, transport then people responding to your poll will think it is something important that they *should* care about. However, come the election the issue will take its place in the public debate alongside issues like the economy, the NHS, or pensions and soon fade to insignificance.

Second, respondents to surveys are not lab rats. You can't blind people to the fact they are taking part in a survey, and people can and will use the question to indicate their support or opposition to a policy, regardless of whether it really would change their vote. 'This would change my vote' is really, for many, a way of saying 'I have an opinion about this.'

The third problem is that people tend to report the answers to such questions in a way that neglects the current party support of those who responded. If you ask a question about whether a policy would make people more or less likely to vote Tory then you'll often find that the majority of people who say the policy would make them more likely to vote Tory are already staunch Conservatives, while the majority of people who say it would make them less likely to vote Tory are people who would never vote Tory anyway. And 'more likely' isn't a very high bar; if a policy proposal has changed someone's likelihood of voting Conservative from, say, 95 per cent to 99 per cent then it has made little substantive difference.

People are also poor judges of what drives their own voting intentions. As many chapters in this book demonstrate, in politics, as in many other areas of life, we do not actually understand our own decision-making processes very well; our decisions are based far more upon our own prejudices, biases and tribal attachments than we would like to imagine.

Despite all these problems, these types of questions are sadly irresistible to journalists. For example, in 2009 44 per cent of people said they'd be much less likely to vote for a party that disconnected the internet for people who shared pirated software; in 2013 22 per cent of people said they would be less likely to vote Labour if Labour members of the House of Lords blocked the passage of the Referendum Bill. In the same year, another poll found 26 per cent of people would be less likely to vote Tory if they made it easier for farmers to shoot foxes for pest control. The silliness of questions like this should be immediately clear: the idea that *several million* people might change their vote because of punishments for file-sharers or rules on when farmers can shoot foxes is patently absurd.

Or take the many polls used to push a second referendum on Brexit, which have claimed that Labour would haemorrhage support to the Liberal Democrats if they did not support a People's Vote. Perhaps, but with 2017 providing a fresh example of a genuine election where Labour sat on the fence over Brexit and successfully campaigned on other issues instead, it is probably best to be somewhat cautious about such claims.

Polls like this reached a nadir with the debate over gay marriage in 2013. For months newspapers treated us to reports claiming that 'Gay marriage could cost Conservatives power', accompanied by poll findings apparently showing that same-sex marriage was costing the Conservatives large chunks of support. In April 2013 a poll in areas with local elections found 23 per cent of people said they were less likely to vote Tory in local elections because of gay marriage, including 26 per cent of people who voted Tory in 2010. (They included 12 per cent of the sample who said they would vote Conservative at the local elections – a case, one assumes, of 'Lord, make me less likely to vote Tory … but not just yet'.) Another poll in January 2013 found 20 per cent of 2010 Tories agreeing that 'I would have considered voting Conservative at the next election but will definitely not if the coalition government legalises same-sex marriage'.

Given the prominence of the debate, YouGov (for whom I work) tried to get round as many of the issues as possible. We hid gay marriage among a longer list of issues and asked people to pick those most likely to influence their vote, then asked those who did say same-sex marriage in which way it would influence them. That found only 7 per cent said that same-sex marriage was a subject that would influence their vote, and by 54 per cent to 44 per cent, that subset of voters said they were *more*, not less, likely to vote for a party that supported gay marriage. The majority of these respondents didn't vote Conservative in 2010 anyway, so these were not the 'lost Tory voters' the media were focusing on. Among 2010 Tory voters, only 4 per cent said same-sex marriage would be an important factor in deciding their vote and that they would be less likely to vote for a party that supported it. That is, one in twenty-five, not one in four, showing that gay marriage was dwarfed by issues like the running of the economy and public services.

Even this probably wasn't an especially *good* measure of the direct impact of gay marriage at the general election, but it was better than the other surveys chasing easy publicity. In the event, the eventual legalisation of gay marriage presumably did not deter that many voters, given the unexpected Tory majority at the 2015 election.

People will always be poor judges of their own motivations and focusing on single issues alone misses out major factors that we know drive voting intentions, such as leadership perceptions and party identification. Voting is too complicated to deal with in one question, and you should probably steer clear of any poll that claims to do so.

FURTHER READING

For a far more solid look at what drives voting intentions based on serious analysis of polling data, look to the work of the British Election Study, most recently 'Brexit or Corbyn? Campaign and Inter-election Vote Switching in the 2017 UK General Election' by Jonathan Mellon et al. (*Parliamentary Affairs*, 2018). While it predates the rise of internet polling, for a more general overview of British political opinion polling the best book remains Nick Moon's *Opinion Polls: History, Theory and Practice* (Manchester University Press, 1999).

—CHAPTER 5—

Information matters: public support for overseas aid

Jennifer van Heerde-Hudson

When asked, British voters will tell you that roughly one in every five pounds spent by the UK government is spent on overseas aid. Europeans estimate aid spending at 10–15 per cent and Americans think – optimistically or pessimistically depending on how you look at it – that 25 per cent of the US federal budget is spent on foreign aid. All of these figures massively overestimate overseas aid spending. In 2018, the UK government spent £14 billion, roughly 1.7 per cent of the national budget, on aid. This does not make the UK unusually stingy. In fact, the UK government is one of only six countries who meet the UN target of spending 0.7 per cent of gross national income on Official Development Assistance: most rich democracies spend less than 1 per cent on aid.

Despite being a generally low-salience issue in British politics, overseas aid divides the public. This is due, in part, to the coalition government's decision to ring-fence aid, alongside NHS spending, despite a wider move towards fiscal 'austerity' during the economic crisis, a policy continued by its successors. And, with the breakdown of the robust cross-party consensus on aid that characterised the past two decades, there are also signs that aid is increasingly dividing elites.

Even with increased public and political attention to aid, British voters continue to substantially overestimate the UK's commitment to poverty reduction. A survey from the Aid Attitudes Tracker project asked respondents two questions: the proportion of the national budget they *thought* the UK government spent on overseas aid, and how much *should* be spent on aid. The average estimate of spending was 18 per cent. Not everyone was completely wrong, however; the modal or most commonly cited estimate was 1 per cent, and more than a third of respondents thought overseas aid spending accounted for less than 5 per cent of total spending. On average, respondents indicated spending should be about half (9 per cent) of what they thought was spent.

For aid advocates, this could be viewed as good news: although the public wildly overestimates aid expenditure, they nevertheless say they would prefer to spend much more than the current 1.7 per cent. It turns out, however, that the public doesn't want to spend very much on overseas aid at all. When given information on *actual* spending levels, the public take the opportunity to restrain spending even further.

Given that more than 80 per cent of people said aid spending accounted for more than 2 per cent of annual expenditure, you might expect that giving people the true figures would boost support for higher aid expenditure. A reasonable hypothesis would be: if John *thinks* that 10 per cent of the budget is spent on aid, 5 per cent *should* be spent, and 1.7 per cent *is* spent, John should support increased aid spending. Likewise, if Julie *thinks* that 10 per cent of the budget is spent on aid, 1 per cent *should* be spent, and 1.7 per cent *is* spent, Julie shouldn't support increased aid spending. But it turns out the public don't think like John or Julie.

In a survey experiment, respondents were randomly assigned to one of seven groups. The control group was prompted only to 'think about the amount of money the UK government spends on overseas aid'. In theory, respondents in this group should favour spending less on aid, if, like those respondents mentioned above, they wildly overestimate actual aid spending. The other six groups were each given accurate information about current aid spending, using a variety of descriptions: the amount in pounds, in percentage terms, both combined, as pounds per £100 spent, and using visual aids.

So what happens to support for overseas aid spending when respondents are told how much is spent on aid? Very little. As the table shows, those in the control group (given no information on aid spending) had roughly the same level of support as those shown how much is spent comparatively, in either a pie or bar chart. Expressing spending as actual expenditure (£11.2 billion at the time of the experiment) or as a percentage of the then budget (1.6 per cent) has no effect on support. Even framing aid in terms of pounds spent per £100 of the total government budget produces no statistically significant change in support for aid spending. In other words, no matter how we talk about aid, the public generally wants to spend less on it.

INFORMATION AND SUPPORT FOR OVERSEAS AID SPENDING

	INCREASE A GREAT DEAL	INCREASE SOMEWHAT	STAY THE SAME	DECREASE SOMEWHAT	DECREASE A GREAT DEAL
Thinking about the amount of money the government spends on overseas aid …	2	11	25	27	35
Thinking about the £11.2 billion …	1	8	26	28	37
Thinking about the 1.6 per cent of the budget …	1	7	30	26	35
Thinking about the 11.2 billion pounds or 1.6 per cent of the budget …	4	5	23	27	41
Of every £100 the government spends, £1.60 is spent on overseas aid …	3	8	25	33	31
The pie chart shows the percentage of the budget …	2	10	29	32	28
The bar chart shows the percentage of the budget …	2	9	25	32	32

Source: YouGov, 2013.

While 'information matters' in the formation of opinion, it isn't the only factor. In the case of overseas aid, there is good evidence to suggest that perceptions of corruption and waste play a big role in driving attitudes and opinions: two-thirds of the British public think that we should not send aid to countries with corrupt governments; more than 90 per cent think every penny of aid should reach its intended targets; and most think a lot of aid spending is 'wasted'. Tackling the views of aid as wasted or likely to wind up in the hands of corrupt politicians would appear to be a prerequisite to increasing support. Second, the public discourse and media portrayal of aid is predominantly negative, and new information can't or simply doesn't override the strong negative images that have already formed in voters' minds. Simply showing voters that the government spends much less than they think on overseas aid is not enough to change their minds.

FURTHER READING

For more on whether information matters see Tom Scotto et al.'s 'We spend how much? Misperceptions, Innumeracy, and Support for the Foreign Aid in the United States and Great Britain' (*Journal of Experimental Political Science*, 2017). A critical assessment of cross-national surveys of public opinion and aid can be found in David Hudson and Jennifer van Heerde-Hudson's 'A Mile Wide and an Inch Deep' (*International Journal of Development Education and Global Learning*, 2012). For more information on the Aid Attitudes Tracker project see: https://devcommslab.org.

CHAPTER 6

Wrong about nearly everything, but still rational: public opinion as a thermostat

Will Jennings

'**B**ritish public wrong about nearly everything, survey shows,' proclaimed a headline in *The Independent* in 2013, reporting findings from an Ipsos MORI survey for the Royal Statistical Society. It found people thought 31 per cent of the population were immigrants, when the actual number was 13 per cent; that 58 per cent of people thought crime was rising, when in fact it was falling; and that people believed that £24 out of every £100 spent on benefits was claimed fraudulently, when the official figure was £0.70.

One of the perennial puzzles about the nature of mass opinion is how, despite the public knowing little about politics, and caring even less about the ebb and flow of public affairs, *collective* public opinion often turns out to be coherent and responsive to events and to new information. An influential line of research takes the view that while individuals may be ill-informed, public opinion in the aggregate is still 'rational', moving in response to events and changes in policy.

Perhaps the most persuasive explanation for this lies in the idea of public opinion as a 'thermostat'. The public may not have a good sense of what the government is actually doing but they are capable of making *relative* judgements of whether there is 'too much' or 'too little' government activity. This is an easier assessment to make than trying to understand the complex details of government policy. Voters simply observe the direction government is moving in, and react in the opposite direction. When policy-makers deliver *more* of something (such as more spending in a particular area), the public's demand for it decreases. When policy-makers deliver *less*, the public's demand increases (so voters react to spending cuts by demanding increased spending). The public regulates government activity like a thermostat regulates room temperature: when politicians turn up the heat, public demand shuts off; when politicians' interest in an issue cools, public anxieties heat up.

This idea of public opinion as a thermostat was developed by Christopher Wlezien using data on the responsiveness of public opinion to spending of the US government on defence, cities, education, the environment, health and welfare. Wlezien's study found substantial feedback from actual spending on the public's relative preference for more or less policy. For defence, for example, he showed that a 1 per cent increase in appropriations led to a reduction of 2.7 per cent in the proportion of the public desiring more over less spending. According to Wlezien, the public sends a consistent and meaningful signal about what it wants to policy-makers.

Similar to its preferences for spending, the public's attention to issues can at times seem capricious – being concerned about crime one month, focusing on the threat of bird flu the next, and turning to petrol prices the next. Yet the topics that are on people's minds are often a good indicator of the degree to which they are a problem. Consider unemployment. The Ipsos MORI survey mentioned earlier found that, on average, the public thought the rate of unemployment was twenty-two out of every hundred people of working age, when the actual number was eight. But plot the proportion of the British public in a given month naming unemployment as 'the most important issue' facing the country against the actual unemployment rate and a very different picture emerges. For the period since 1979, public attention tracks the official unemployment figures remarkably closely. Similar patterns are observed for the rate of inflation and the number of working days lost due to industrial action as well, each of which also moves in parallel with the relative emphasis placed on the issue by the public.

UNEMPLOYMENT RATE AND SHARE OF VOTERS RATING UNEMPLOYMENT AS THE MOST IMPORTANT ISSUE FACING THE COUNTRY

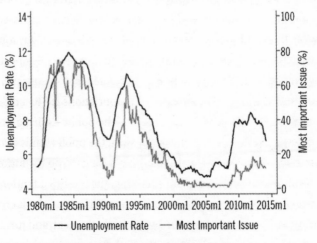

Source: Ipsos MORI (most important issue), Office for National Statistics (unemployment).

So what underpins this process of opinion formation? It is possible to outline several ideas about why *uninformed* or *inattentive* mass opinion may still be responsive to changes in policy or policy outcomes.

The first is simply that preferences or the problem status of issues are *relative*. People want more or less spending, or consider a particular issue to be more or less important than other issues. They do not need to know precisely the amount of policy they want to hold such preferences, just as someone who feels too cold doesn't need to know the precise temperature they want to be before putting the heating on.

The second is that on most issues the public receives a substantial amount of information either directly or indirectly about whether they are receiving more or less government activity in particular areas. Job figures, inflation, train delays, increases or cuts to public spending on hospitals are all regularly reported in the media. Of course in some areas the processing of this information can become severely distorted, to the extent that the relationship breaks down. Take crime, for example, where there is a long-standing gap between public perceptions of crime and the actual crime rate. Widespread distrust of official statistics means public opinion is not responsive to changes in policy or outcomes, or lags well behind them.

The third is that changes in aggregate opinion are not necessarily driven by the average citizen, who knows or cares little about policy, but whose 'errors' about policy at the individual level tend to cancel out in the aggregate. Movements in mass opinion can instead be driven by relatively small sections of the population ('opinion leaders') who possess the cognitive capacity to adjust their opinion in response to policy change in meaningful and systematic ways.

Despite people being poor judges of the actual level of policy and often holding incoherent views on issues, the ebbs and flows of mass opinion tend to reflect meaningful responses to events and to the rise and fall of problems on the agenda. It follows, then, that public opinion can exhibit 'rational' patterns of movement in relative terms, even when it is wrong about nearly everything in terms of the specifics.

FURTHER READING

The Royal Statistical Society study was reported in Jonathan Paige's 'British public wrong about nearly everything, survey shows' (*The Independent*, 9 July 2013); multiple further examples can be found in Bobby Duffy's *Perils of Perception* (Atlantic, 2018). The idea of the public as a thermostat comes from Christopher Wlezien's 'The Public as Thermostat: dynamics of Preferences for Spending' (*American Journal of Political Science*, 2005). The characteristics of polls about the 'most important issue' are discussed in Will Jennings and Christopher Wlezien's 'Distinguishing between Most Important Problems and Issues?' (*Public Opinion Quarterly*, 2011). The argument that aggregate opinion is driven by opinion leaders is put forward in *The Macro Polity* by Robert Erikson et al. (Cambridge University Press, 2002).

CHAPTER 7

Rash promises and tears: exit polls

John Curtice

They have become part of the folklore of British election night. 'I'll run naked down Whitehall if that turns out to be true,' wrote Iain Dale, well-known radio host and book publisher, on the night of the 2010 election.

'If this poll is right, I will publicly eat my hat,' said the former Liberal Democrat leader Paddy Ashdown in 2015.

Why such rash promises? In both cases, disbelief at the results of the exit poll that the three main broadcasting organisations, BBC, ITV and Sky, had just published.

Their scepticism was, perhaps, understandable. After an election campaign that had seen a dramatic if gradually fading bounce in the Liberal Democrats' poll ratings, the 2010 poll was predicting that the party would win four fewer seats than in 2005.

In 2015, every opinion poll pointed to a close contest between Conservative and Labour, yet the exit poll was anticipating that, with 316 seats, the incumbent Conservative Prime Minister was home and dry, albeit perhaps without an overall majority.

In practice, the 2010 and 2015 exit polls proved much more

accurate than either Iain Dale or Paddy Ashdown had anticipated. In 2010, the Liberal Democrats ended up with fifty-seven
seats, slightly fewer even than the exit poll anticipated, while the
forecast tally of 307 seats for the Conservatives was exactly right.
Meanwhile, in 2015, the Conservatives performed even better
than the exit poll anticipated, winning 331 seats and an overall
majority of twelve.

There were more shock waves in 2017. Most polls anticipated
that Theresa May would secure a significantly increased majority.
But the exit poll dramatically, and correctly, suggested she would
find herself without a majority at all. There were no rash promises
this time – just the gentle trickle of a tear down the Prime Minister's face when her husband told her the bad news.

So, what is this polling exercise that has given rise to so many
surprises? An exit poll approaches people as they leave a sample
of polling stations across the country and asks them to complete
a mock ballot paper to indicate how they have just voted. The
results are then collated and analysed with a view to predicting
at 10 p.m. – when the polling stations close – what the overall
outcome in seats will be.

It sounds like an easy exercise. Ask voters how they have voted,
add up the totals for each party, and then work out how many
seats each party is likely to obtain as a result.

In practice, it is far from easy. For a start, no organisation can
afford to cover all of the 40,000 or so polling stations at which
people vote. They have to select a small sample of stations at which
to conduct their interviews. However, unlike in most other countries, general elections in the UK are not counted, and the results
are not published, polling station by polling station. Consequently

it is virtually impossible to know whether or not any particular sample of polling stations is likely to reflect the behaviour of the country as a whole.

Exit polls have therefore given up trying to find such a set of stations. Instead, the approach nowadays is based on the observation that although the level of support for each political party varies considerably from one constituency to another, the extent to which the *change* in a party's level of support varies from one seat to another is much less, and is thus more likely to be estimated correctly by any set of polling stations. Thus rather than attempting to estimate each party's share of the vote, the exit poll attempts to estimate how much each party's vote is up or down since the last election and then applies those estimates to the actual result last time.

But how can that possibly be done if we do not know the result in each polling station last time around? Well, the one set of polling stations for which we do have an estimate of how people voted last time are the stations at which an exit poll was conducted last time around. So if, wherever possible, the exit poll is conducted at exactly the same places as last time, we can derive an estimate of how much each party's vote is up or down by comparing the tally of votes for each party this time with the equivalent tally last time.

There are a couple of other crucial stages to the process. First, a party's support may systematically go up or down rather more in certain kinds of constituencies than in others. That could have an impact on how many seats it looks likely to win (because, for example, it means its vote is holding up better or worse in marginal seats). The exit poll analysts thus have to try to identify any systematic variation in how much each party's vote is changing, and, if necessary, produce different estimates of change for different kinds of constituencies.

Second, the exit poll's estimate of how much each party's vote will rise or fall in each constituency is subject to sampling error. So if we estimate that two parties are in a close race for first place, we should be wary of assuming that whichever party is expected to be (narrowly) ahead will definitely win the seat. It is more realistic to say that both parties have a 50 per cent or so chance of winning. Consequently, for each party an estimate is derived of the probability that they will win each of the 633 seats in Great Britain; the total number of seats a party is forecast to win is then the sum of those probabilities across all seats. This feature proved especially crucial in enabling the poll to produce an accurate estimate of Labour's majority in 2005: there were lots of seats where the party was only just the favourite to come first, many of which it subsequently failed to win.

Even then, there are still plenty of risks. Not all voters are willing to take part in exit polls, and the results will be skewed if one party's supporters are more reluctant to do so. Sometimes the geographical area served by a polling station is changed, making it impossible to compare the result with last time. Around 15 per cent of British voters vote by post rather than go to a polling station, and they could possibly behave differently. Meanwhile, most voters vote in the early evening of polling day, leaving very little time to analyse and spot the crucial patterns in the data.

Yet, despite all these risks, recent exit polls have proven surprisingly accurate – as Paddy Ashdown acknowledged when, on the day after the 2015 election, he was presented by the BBC with a marzipan hat for him to eat. However, Iain Dale has still to keep his promise!

FURTHER READING

Full details of the method used by the exit poll are to be found in John Curtice and David Firth's 'Exit Polling in a Cold Climate: the BBC–ITV Experience in 2005 (with discussion)' (*Journal of the Royal Statistical Society Series A*, 2008). An equivalent analysis and description of the 2010 poll is to be found in 'Confounding the Commentators: How the 2010 Exit Poll got it (more or less) right' by John Curtice et al. (*Journal of Elections, Public Opinion and Parties*, 2011). A brief description of the most recent exit poll in 2017 is provided by John Curtice and colleagues in 'Surprise, surprise (again): The 2017 British general election exit poll' (*Significance*, 2017).

'No part of the education of a politician is more indispensable than the fighting of elections.'

– WINSTON CHURCHILL, *GREAT CONTEMPORARIES*, 1937

—CHAPTER 8—

Mondeo meh: the myth of target voters

James Morris

In the run-up to every election, newspapers fill with articles about the handful of voters that will supposedly swing the result – 'soccer moms', 'NASCAR dads', 'Worcester women', even 'pebbledash people'. Occasionally this analysis is useful. Normally it is not. In the 2016 US presidential election, all but eight states shifted in the same direction – to the right. In the past six UK elections, 84 per cent of demographic groups swung in the same way as the population as a whole. The notable exception to this pattern in the UK is class – where in the past two elections middle-class groups have swung to Labour at the same time as more working-class groups have swung away from the party.

A common trick to make a target group sound worth focusing on is to highlight what is distinctive about them, at the expense of what is important. For example, *Guardian* readers are more likely to be Labour voters (73 per cent voted Labour in 2017) than *Mail* readers (17 per cent). But the *Mail* sells nine times as many copies as *The Guardian*, more than enough to compensate for the difference. If you want to target Labour voters, the *Mail* reaches more of them than *The Guardian*.

Another technique is to present polling results comparing one subgroup with another, without mentioning specific numbers. It allows you to say things like 'older men were twice as likely as younger women to think the Conservatives are on the side of ordinary people'. This sounds significant until you realise that the numbers in question (from a poll I carried out for the TUC) are 6 per cent and 3 per cent.

So why do we get all this fuss about Mondeo Man and his friends whenever an election rolls around?

It is partly because establishing the importance of particular groups can be politically useful. Campaigning organisations have a particular interest in arguing that their client group will be decisive and therefore make hyperbolic claims about the group's electoral influence to attract attention from the parties and the press.

Take as an example the claim from Operation Black Vote that 'the black vote can decide the 2015 general election'. This was based on analysis which found 168 seats where ethnic minority voters outnumbered the majority of the sitting MP. Operation Black Vote is a great organisation that has achieved a lot, but this argument for electoral significance is equally true of every demographic group in those seats which was at least as populous as ethnic minority communities. It would apply to women, men, the over-forties, the under-forties, mums, dads, grandparents, racists, anti-racists, believers in astrology, pet-owners and so on.

Thinking of electoral targets in terms of demographic niches leads parties to develop policies aimed at each niche. This is exactly the effect that lobbyists want, but it is not a ticket to electoral success. As Labour found in 2015, firing popular rent cap policies at young people in Harlow and popular energy policies at older people in Cleethorpes made no difference when Labour wasn't able to boost trust on the fundamentals of leadership and economic credibility. Lots of hyper-targeted policy, even if it is very popular with the target audiences, is not enough to secure victory.

Parties that successfully use targeting use it in three ways.

First, they use geographic targets: marginal seats, swing districts and battleground states. This form of targeting is absolutely fundamental to campaign design in constituency-focused political systems. Resources are poured into districts where an extra pound might make a difference and kept out of places where a party is confident of victory or defeat. This is not without risks, as illustrated by Hillary Clinton's 2016 campaign, which put a lot of effort into ever more sophisticated modelling of voters, but didn't bother targeting several of the states that swung the election due to a misplaced confidence that these were 'safe'.

Second, successful micro-targeted appeals curate and tailor the overall message but do not try to create a separate message. The 2016 Democratic primary was a great example of this point. Bernie Sanders's strength with young people did not come through specific youth-oriented policy offers but because his overall message attacking corporate greed and calling for radical change resonated particularly strongly with young people. Similarly, the Brexit campaign's success with older voters came about through linking specific messages to the idea of 'taking back control', not focusing on issues that just older people care about. Individualised messages on Facebook and other digital platforms fit within these overall frameworks and amplify the most compelling elements for individuals.

Third, parties use targeting as a form of internal communication. This is partly about projecting sophistication to political commentators. Shouting about how a campaign will use 'big data' is often enough to earn favourable coverage. More importantly, it is about explaining to party volunteers that the people they are trying to persuade have different priorities and values to your typical activist.

One of the most famous target groups in British politics was Mondeo Man. According to Tony Blair: 'His dad voted Labour. He used to vote Labour, too. But he'd bought his own house now. He'd set up his own business. He was doing very nicely. His instincts were to get on in life.' Parse that: he's a man (49 per cent of the population); from a family where at least one parent voted Labour (back when 90 per cent either voted Labour or Conservative); owns his own home (65 per cent of the population); self-employed (so could be in the trades, or running a shop or a small company), and his instincts tell him to work hard and succeed (almost everyone). In short, Mondeo Man was a pretty normal kind of a guy in the types of marginal seat Labour was trying to win. It says less about New Labour's psephological genius and more about the peculiar internal politics of the party that this kind of person was a stretching target.

FURTHER READING

For more on how data driven targeted campaigning can shift the vote see *The Victory Lab* (Broadway Books, 2012) by Sasha Issenberg. For a more sceptical take, have a look at *The Gamble* (Princeton University Press, 2014) by John Sides and Lynn Vavreck. Justin Fisher's paper 'Constituency Campaigning at the 2015 General Election' looks at local campaign effects, while the co-editor of this volume has a tome, *The British General Election of 2015* (Palgrave Macmillan, 2016) that gives an insight into what the parties themselves think decided the 2015 campaign. For a look at how big-picture social and demographic changes matter more than the decisions campaigns make, read *Democracy for Realists: Why Elections Do Not Produce Responsive Government* by Christopher Achen and Larry Bartels (Princeton University Press, 2016).

CHAPTER 9

The surprise of June 2016: how public opinion changes during referendum campaigns

Alan Renwick

When David Cameron pledged in January 2013 to call a referendum on the UK's membership of the European Union, he did so because he expected to win. Polls at the time put Remain ahead. Furthermore, Cameron expected that gap to grow. He and those around him believed the lesson of past referendums to be that, as polling day approaches, voters get cold feet about change and revert to the comfort of the status quo.

That had been the pattern in the referendum two years before on Westminster electoral reform. Early polls had put the change option well ahead. But voters ultimately plumped for the status quo, by a decisive 68–32 margin. Relentless sloganeering that the proposed reform would be complicated, cost more and somehow violate democratic principles had ground down voters' early enthusiasm for shaking things up.

But the Brexit referendum did not go according to plan. Opinion did not shift towards the status quo: in fact, it drifted the other way. Average Remain support across 160 polls published in the twelve months before the vote was 51.7 per cent, 3.6 percentage points higher than the final result.

This was one of the most consequential miscalculations ever made by a British politician. In expecting a shift to the status quo, did Cameron and his circle misread history? Or did Brexit buck the trend?

There were 291 state-wide referendums in stable democracies between 1990 and 2018. In the twelve months before each of these, there were a total of 1,753 opinion polls relating to the referendum issue. The analysis here covers the 117 referendums for which we have three or more polls.

CHANGE IN SUPPORT FOR THE STATUS QUO FROM OPINION POLLS TO ACTUAL VOTE (PERCENTAGE POINTS)

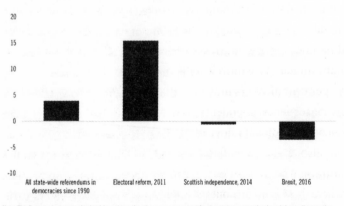

Note: The figures shown are obtained by subtracting the average support for the status quo option in opinion polls over the twelve months before each vote (excluding 'Don't knows') from the actual support for the status quo option in the referendum.

The chart opposite compares support for the status quo in the polls and in the actual vote. The first column shows the overall pattern across the 117 referendums. Cameron turns out to have been right about the general trend: on average, support shifted by 3.9 percentage points towards the status quo. The UK's 2011 referendum on electoral reform turns out to have been an unusually strong case of this: support for the status quo was 15.4 percentage points higher in the final tally than in the polls over the preceding year. By contrast, the Scottish independence vote in 2014 saw no overall move, while the 2016 Brexit referendum swung the other way.

The general trend is not just the product of some freak outliers. Of these 117 referendums, eighty-one saw opinion shift towards the status quo; only thirty-six away. What's more, the overall average may actually understate the expected effect, because of important differences between countries in how referendums are run. Ireland, for example, experienced an average shift towards the status quo of 8.8 percentage points across nineteen referendums with sufficient data, whereas the average move across ten referendums in Italy was 9.3 percentage points *away from* the status quo. A key difference between these countries is that most referendums in Italy, unlike those in Ireland, apply a turnout threshold: at least 50 per cent of voters must cast a ballot for the result to be valid. In consequence, opponents of change who are behind in the polls encourage voters to boycott the vote. This invalidates the result but also artificially inflates support for change as a proportion of those who do turn out. When we focus only on referendums where there is no turnout threshold to distort the voting, the average shift towards the status quo rises to 6.2 percentage points.

Putting it another way, had the Brexit vote played out like the average referendum with no turnout threshold, Remain would have won by 57.9 to 42.1 per cent. The politics of the years since the vote – and of many years to come – would have been vastly different.

Yet this overall trend should not be exaggerated: the Brexit vote was one of nearly a third of all the referendums covered here – 36 of 117 – where opinion moved in favour of change. Our task is to understand why these cases differ from the rest.

The first explanation is 'reversion point reversal', which happens when campaigns manage to change perceptions of the status quo, so cautious voters are persuaded that the best way of protecting what they already have is to vote for the change option on the ballot paper. That was clearly central to the Brexit referendum. The Leave campaign's key slogan – 'take back control' – appealed to the idea that leaving the EU was actually a reversion to a better past.

If you go through campaign materials and reports from all the referendums in our sample, you find a marked difference between the sixty-six cases where arguments shifting perceptions of the status quo were present and the fifty-one where they were absent. With reversion point reversal, the average shift towards the status quo is very small (1.9 points on average). Without it, the pattern is much stronger (6.3 points).

The second factor is the emergence of anti-establishment bandwagons. It is hard to detect these cross-nationally, but such an effect again clearly mattered in 2016. Many Leave voters were protesting against an elite that they felt ignored by. They became ever more determined to defy the siren calls of 'Project Fear' as the campaign progressed.

Overall, then, Cameron and his colleagues were right: referendums generally see a shift of opinion towards the status quo as polling day approaches. But they were incautious in assuming that such a move was guaranteed: in fact, about a third of referendums go the other way. That is especially likely if voting for the change option can successfully be portrayed as the best way to preserve cherished features of the status quo or if an anti-establishment bandwagon can whip up disgruntlement with ruling elites. Both factors were strong in 2016, and so British politics was changed for ever.

FURTHER READING

For detailed analysis of opinion change in the Brexit referendum see 'The UK's Referendum on EU Membership of June 2016: How Expectations of Brexit's Impact Affected the Outcome' by Stephen Fisher and Alan Renwick (*Acta Politica*, 2018). For more on that vote see John Curtice's 'Why Leave Won the UK's EU Referendum' (*Journal of Common Market Studies*, 2017) and Sara Hobolt's 'The Brexit Vote: A Divided Nation, a Divided Continent' (*Journal of European Public Policy*, 2016). For earlier evidence on opinion change in referendums see Lawrence LeDuc's chapter in David M. Farrell and Rüdiger Schmitt-Beck (eds), *Do Political Campaigns Matter? Campaign Effects in Elections and Referendums* (Routledge, 2001).

—CHAPTER 10—

Playing on home turf: the importance of issue ownership

James Dennison

Voters consistently rank some parties as better at handling certain issues than others. In the United States, for example, voters regularly name the Republicans as the best party to deal with security and crime, whereas the Democrats are ranked as the best party on social security and education. When voters habitually think of a party as being better equipped to deal with an issue, we say the party 'owns' the issue. If the issues that a party owns are those that a voter cares about, this should dramatically boost the voter's chance of voting for that party – voters should gravitate to the parties thought to be best at solving the problems that matter most to them.

The distribution of issue ownership tends to be fairly stable across time, both because voters' perceptions about parties are difficult to change and because of the considerable resources that parties invest into maintaining their reputations on issues where they are strong. Moreover, parties have an incentive to emphasise the importance of their owned issues in order to fully exploit their political value.

Historic and long-running examples of issue ownership in the UK include Labour on health and education and the Conservatives on the economy and crime, as evidenced by hundreds of polls over the last decades. But changes do happen. In the 1990s, following the European Exchange Rate Mechanism crisis, the Conservative Party's competence on economic matters began to be questioned just at the time that Labour was committing itself to a more moderate economic approach – and the result was a rare shift in issue ownership. More recently, the Conservatives, who had consistently owned immigration since the 1970s, lost the issue to the populist right UK Independence Party (UKIP).

BEST PARTY TO HANDLE IMMIGRATION, 2010–15

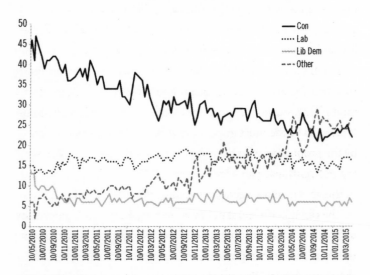

Source: YouGov Issues Tracker.

In just five years, over the course of the 2010–15 parliament, the Conservatives went from having a thirty-point lead as the best party to handle immigration to being behind UKIP and only 10 points ahead of Labour. Why did this happen? Five years of a Conservative-led government presiding over high immigration levels despite pledging to bring them down did lasting damage to the party's reputation on the issue: a majority of voters in 2015 blamed the government for high levels of immigration and believed that the party neither cared about the issue nor wanted to reduce immigration. Furthermore, a majority of voters came to believe that David Cameron's party would be unsuccessful at reducing immigration even if it tried.

This loss of ownership was particularly harmful to the Conservatives because immigration was then at the top of the political agenda. In December 2015, 63 per cent of voters believed that immigration was one of the top three issues affecting the UK, far ahead of the economy on 39 per cent. As in a number of other European countries, a populist right party seems to have gained ownership over one of the major prizes of contemporary politics. The translation of ownership into votes is fairly clear. Simply multiplying the proportion of the electorate who considered immigration to be the most important issue in May 2015 (52 per cent), by the proportion who believed UKIP would be best on that issue (27 per cent), gave an accurate prediction for UKIP's vote share in the 2015 general election: just under 14 per cent.

The capture of a major policy issue was a particularly impressive feat for UKIP, not just in terms of their swiftness in doing so and the issue's relative importance, but because UKIP was not one of the major parties. By way of comparison, the Liberal Democrats

– with a much longer history and much larger Westminster presence – were *never* ranked as the best party to deal with a major policy issue between 2005 and 2015, though they did come close on education and taxation prior to the 2010 general election.

Moreover, despite UKIP's recent steep electoral decline, in late 2018 around 15 per cent of Britons *still* saw UKIP (a party polling at under 5 per cent at this point) as the best party to deal with immigration. It seems unlikely that the Conservatives will be able to recover the levels of dominance on immigration they once had, at least for some time, because people often evaluate immigration policy via immigration levels, which will remain difficult for the British government to effectively control in many of the possible post-EU scenarios.

In fact, the Conservatives now campaign far less on immigration than they have done in the past and, rather than waste resources on an issue that they do not own, have instead shifted their focus to the issues they do own, such as the economy and, for a period after the EU referendum, Europe. Therefore, aside from UKIP and the upstart Brexit Party, no major British party currently has an incentive to campaign on immigration. Despite the subject's high salience with many voters (it is still typically listed as one of the most important issues by at least a quarter of the electorate in 2019), a new electoral equilibrium has arisen that replicates the campaign of 2015 in its relative quiet on the subject. Immigration is, in some respects, essentially 'parked' as an issue to campaign on, with polls not yet reflecting a Conservative recovery on the subject. Ironically, therefore, public discontent over immigration was so strong that it led to the emergence of new parties, yet, now that the damage to issue ownership has been done on the subject, the best thing the established parties can do is to let those new parties do all the talking.

FURTHER READING

The concepts and previous empirical findings on 'issue ownership' are developed in 'Introduction: Issue Ownership' by Jonas Lefevere et al. (*West European Politics*, 2015) and Éric Bélanger and Bonnie Meguid's 'Issue Salience, Issue Ownership and Issue-Based Vote Choice' (*Electoral Studies*, 2008). For UKIP and immigration see James Dennison and Matthew Goodwin's 'Immigration, Issue Ownership and the Rise of UKIP' (*Parliamentary Affairs*, 2015).

CHAPTER 11

Looking good for election day: do attractive candidates do better?

Caitlin Milazzo

We use first impressions every day to judge the people we encounter. Often based largely or solely on someone's appearance, these snap judgements help us to determine who we consider competent or trustworthy. As a result, first impressions tend to predict a wide range of behaviours. Attractiveness, in particular, is a powerful attribute. Teachers who are perceived to be more attractive receive more positive student evaluations, even when the teachers are evaluated using only short video clips with no sound. Similarly, attractive university professors tend to receive evaluations that are, on average, nearly a point higher on a five-point scale. Attractive individuals are more likely to receive assistance from strangers, and attractive children tend to receive more attention from adults. Attractiveness also conveys a variety of benefits in business: individuals who are perceived to be attractive are more likely to be hired and promoted, and they tend to receive higher incomes.

Such superficial judgements should, of course, play no role in politics. Except that there is considerable evidence that they do. In a famous study from the United States, Todorov and his colleagues showed that US congressional candidates who were judged more competent in the laboratory (based on as little as thirty-three milliseconds of exposure to photos) were the real election winners about 70 per cent of the time. The effect of appearance is by no means limited to the US; studies document the relationship between appearance and election results in countries around the world. Indeed, the effect of appearance is so significant that one recent study was able to predict French election results using the judgements that Swiss children made from looking at photos of the candidates.

There are many things we might infer about political candidates based on their appearance. Do they appear to be competent? Do they appear to be honest or caring? All of these are traits that people value in their political leaders. However, unlike these traits, attractiveness conveys no meaningful information about a candidate's ability to represent his or her constituents. And yet studies document a relationship between perceptions of attractiveness and electoral success in Australia, Brazil, Canada, Finland, Germany, Mexico and Switzerland. British elections are no exception. Attractiveness has been shown to give an edge in races where the candidates were members of the opposite sex. Women, in particular, are more likely to prefer an attractive candidate. Attractiveness is also a predictor of success in local elections where voters tend to care less about the outcome.

One study of the 2010 British general election asked undergraduates from an American university to evaluate real British candidates using quickly formed first impressions of a photograph of the candidate's face. To minimise the differences between the photographs, all 150 photographs featured candidates facing forward, all the photographs and faces were roughly the same size and resolution, and all the candidates were smiling. The photographs were paired according to actual electoral races in which the candidates ran against each other. The students were shown two images for each election, of the winner and the second place candidate, with each picture being shown one at a time for less than one second each. Participants had thirty seconds to decide which candidate they thought was the more attractive of the pair.

There were many races where the students had a clear preference on which candidate was more attractive. Conservative candidates were rated as being more attractive 58 per cent of the time, compared with 41 per cent for Labour candidates and 49 per cent for Liberal Democrat candidates. In addition, students were less likely to find incumbent MPs attractive. These differences may be due to the age of the candidates, as the incumbents tend to be older than the challengers, and in general the study did find that students tended to rate younger candidates as being more attractive; candidates younger than forty years old were, on average, rated as being the more attractive of the pair by 59 per cent of participants, while the percentage dropped to 34 per cent for candidates older than sixty. This is perhaps unsurprising given that the average age of the students was only twenty years.

More surprisingly, however, these perceptions of attractiveness predicted 58 per cent of these election contests. And in close races – those decided by less than 5 per cent of the votes – attractiveness successfully predicted the outcomes of almost three-quarters

(72 per cent) of the elections. Remember that this was using only American students' judgements about the candidates' attractiveness, so the accuracy of this prediction is particularly surprising, as they were unlikely to know anything else about the politicians they were rating.

What exactly is the payoff of being deemed the more attractive candidate? To find this out, the authors calculated the difference in the percentage of votes received by a candidate who was rated as being attractive by 25 per cent of students versus a candidate who is rated as being more attractive by 75 per cent of the students. They found that the more attractive candidate was predicted to have more than a 2 percentage point advantage over their less attractive opponent, even after taking into account the candidate's party and their party's vote share in the constituency in the previous election, as well as the candidate's campaign spending, gender, age, and whether they were an incumbent MP. In the grand scheme of things, 2 percentage points might not seem like much. But in many elections – including 2010, 2015 and 2017 – 2 percentage points can be the difference between a stable majority and a vulnerable government. For example, in 2017, fifty constituencies were decided by less than 2 per cent of votes, and the Conservative Party needed fewer than ten additional seats to gain a majority in Parliament. All of a sudden a difference of 2 percentage points does not seem so small.

FURTHER READING

More information about the findings and the study presented here can be found in Kyle Mattes and Caitlin Milazzo's 'Pretty Faces, Marginal Races: Predicting

Election Outcomes Using Positive and Negative Trait Assessments of British Parliamentary Candidate Images' (*Electoral Studies*, 2014). The methodology used in this study was first developed by Alexander Todorov et al. – see 'Inferences of Competence from Faces Predict Election Outcomes' (*Science*, 2005) – who used rapidly determined first impressions of candidate competence to explain US Congressional outcomes. For information on the role of first impressions see 'Very First Impressions' by Moshe Bar et al. (*Emotion*, 2006) and Ingrid R. Olson and Christy Marshuetz's 'Facial Attractiveness is Appraised in a Glance' (*Emotion*, 2005). There are also a number of other interesting studies about the role of candidate traits in British elections, including 'Ballot Photographs as Cues in Low-Information Elections' by Susan Banducci et al. (*Political Psychology*, 2008), and a series of papers by Mark Shephard and Rob Johns, including their 'Facing the Voters: The Potential Impact of Ballot Paper Photographs' (*Political Studies*, 2011).

CHAPTER 12

Worth the paper they're written on: party manifestos

Nicholas Allen

A head of the 2015 British general election, Labour leader Ed Miliband unveiled a giant limestone slab on which were engraved six key pledges. Had Labour won the election, the widely lampooned 'Ed Stone' was to have served as an unavoidable reminder of the party's commitments. Yet Miliband's accompanying promise to 'restore faith in politics by delivering what we promised at this general election' was doomed to fail, because even if Labour had delivered on the Ed Stone pledges in full, most voters probably wouldn't have believed it.

Most voters just take it for granted that governments renege on their election manifesto commitments. They suspect that politicians will say almost anything to get elected, including making promises they know they cannot keep. In survey after survey, only small minorities of voters think that parties do what they say they will.

Yet like so much conventional wisdom, popular beliefs about

election pledges are mostly wrong. Winning parties do implement the bulk of their manifesto promises. Research suggests that
since 1945 British governments that held office for at least four
years tended to fulfil around four-fifths of their manifesto pledges.
That they did so is less surprising than it might appear. Manifestos underpin the mandate theory of democracy: a government's
right to implement its policies is coupled with an obligation to do
so. Partly for this reason, political parties usually devote a great
deal of time and energy to policy-review exercises, which tend
to filter out impossible commitments. Once elected, ministers
face consistent pressure from within and outside their party to
deliver. It doesn't matter if voters didn't read or don't remember
past manifesto pledges; journalists and opponents do – and will
soon remind voters if the government fails to fulfil them.

The moral authority of manifesto pledges and especially the fear
of being seen to break them can be constraining. The restrictions
imposed by David Cameron's 2015 manifesto were among the factors that drove Theresa May's decision to seek an early election in
2017. The same sense of fear can even constrain parties in opposition. A number of Labour MPs felt bound to support Brexit and
resist calls for a second referendum because their party's 2017 manifesto committed them to accepting the outcome of the 2016 vote.

Of course, all governments fail to do some of the things they
said they would, and also end up doing things they said they would
not do. Sometimes circumstances require parties to rethink their
plans. In its 2005 manifesto, Labour promised not to raise the top
rate of income tax until at least after the next election. After the
2008 financial crisis, it felt it had to do just that. The Liberal Democrats pledged in 2010 to 'scrap unfair university tuition fees'. As

part of the give and take of being in coalition, the party's leadership felt obliged to vote in favour of allowing fees to rise from £3,000 to £9,000.

Expecting politicians to keep all promises would make politics impossible and bad government more likely. Manifestos are wide-ranging blueprints for government, and much of the policy detail can only be worked out when in office. For these reasons, most manifesto pledges tend to be relatively general. According to one study, only 40 per cent of pledges in winning-party manifestos between 1945 and 2001 were of the specific or detailed variety.

Indeed, this is one of the reasons why there is this clash between the public's perception that parties regularly renege on their promises and academics' belief that they tend to keep them. Researchers tend to focus on matching winning parties' activity to specific manifesto commitments where it is possible to make objective judgements as to whether or not an action was taken or a goal achieved. They exclude the rhetorical flourishes that may well raise voters' expectations but which do not commit parties unambiguously to certain actions or goals. Academics also give some credit to governments for partially fulfilling pledges, whereas most voters are probably less charitable. And researchers tend to treat all manifesto pledges equally, even though they clearly vary in significance. For most voters, the fulfilment of a dozen minor promises will almost certainly be eclipsed by the breaking of one centrally important pledge.

Then there are the many promises made by politicians that are not included in manifestos, such as David Cameron's 2009 assurance that the National Health Service would suffer 'no more of those pointless reorganisations that aim for change but instead bring chaos'. Within three years, his government had legislated to do just that. (Ironically, it was the 2010 Conservative manifesto that reneged on Cameron's assurance, by committing the party to implement 'a reform plan to make the changes the NHS needs' – and so the government's Health and Social Care Bill was simultaneously both the keeping of a manifesto promise and the breaking of Cameron's earlier pledge.) Although there is no systematic study of them, non-manifesto promises are probably more likely to be broken, partly because the process of drafting manifestos tends to expose parties' plans to better internal scrutiny, and partly because non-manifesto promises are not seen as part of a government's mandate. Yet, for most journalists and voters, a broken promise is a broken promise, whether or not it was in the manifesto.

While politicians don't always help themselves – proclaiming their own trustworthiness while denigrating their opponents' – the pervasive sense that parties break their election promises is also down to factors largely beyond their control. They have to contend with high levels of generalised public distrust, which predisposes voters to assume the worst about them, and negative media coverage, which serves to reinforce it. Stories celebrating manifesto pledges fulfilled don't sell newspapers. Articles listing and denigrating a government's broken promises do.

For all these reasons, politicians have a reputation for breaking their promises. Given that this reputation is likely to persist, it is worth reflecting on some of the consequences for both the study and the practice of British democracy. For a start, voters' beliefs about political promises highlight a divide between political science and everyday views of politics. By focusing narrowly on the measurable, in this case specific pledges, academics sometimes overlook what matters most to voters.

More importantly, the scepticism surrounding manifestos arguably weakens the foundations underpinning the mandate theory of democracy. It is harder for winning parties to claim legitimacy for their programmes after an election if most voters did not believe in the sincerity of their promises before it. As illustrated by the Ed Stone experience, politicians are now forced to go to ever greater lengths to convince voters of their sincerity. Such stunts may only serve to fuel voters' suspicions.

FURTHER READING

Useful studies of manifesto pledge fulfilment include Judith Bara's 'A Question of Trust: Implementing Party Manifestos' (*Parliamentary Affairs*, 2005) and Robert Thomson et al.'s 'The Fulfillment of Parties' Election Pledges: A Comparative Study on the Impact of Power Sharing' (*American Journal of Political Science*, 2017). Elin Naurin explores the 'pledge puzzle' using evidence from Sweden in *Election Promises, Party Behaviour and Voter Perceptions* (Palgrave Macmillan, 2011), while Jonathan Mellon et al. examine the importance of weighting pledges by voters' perceptions of their importance in 'Which Promises Actually Matter? Understanding Promissory Representation with Conjoint Analysis of Election Pledges' (2018).

—CHAPTER 13—

Signed, sealed, delivered… Testing politicians' responsiveness to voters

Rebecca McKee

When people are asked who they trust, politicians come well down the list. The Ipsos MORI Veracity Index in 2018 showed that over 90 per cent say they trust doctors and nurses to tell the truth but less than one in five trust a politician to do so, placing them even lower than estate agents. A full 50 per cent of people in the 2019 Audit of Political Engagement said that the main parties and politicians do not care about people like them, and just 34 per cent had confidence in MPs to act in the national interest. This lack of trust co-exists alongside substantial disillusionment with politics. Results from the 2017 Eurobarometer put the United Kingdom in the bottom quarter of all European Union countries in terms of public interest in politics. In response to one question included in the 2015 British Election Survey, just a third of BAME respondents believed that their MP would help if they wrote to them about an issue.

Yet we know from other research that MPs spend a great deal

of time responding to the concerns of their constituents – and the time they spend on this has increased over recent decades. Many MPs now report working up to seventy hours per week, with a substantial amount of that time spent engaging with constituents. MPs are now more accessible than ever. Almost all have their own website; around 90 per cent have a Twitter account. Then there is email. No longer is it necessary for a constituent to draft a letter, find a stamp and post it. Instead, they can send a message from their smartphone in an instant.

In the run-up to the 2015 general election, I conducted an experiment to assess how responsive MPs were to their constituents. MPs were sent emails from a 'constituent' who had recently moved to the area and wanted to register to vote and was asking for information on how best to do it. This was at a time when there were widespread concerns that the new voter registration system could lead to the removal of 'missing millions' from the electoral register. The question was clear, on a salient issue, and it required only a simple answer, which any MPs' office should have been able to provide.

The good news, given the low expectations that many voters have of their MPs, was that the response rate to these emails was remarkably high. Some 89 per cent of emails generated a response, with 70 per cent coming back within a day. The responses varied in quality: some directed the constituent to the official websites (aboutmyvote.co.uk, gov.uk/register-to-vote), but others gave no discernible information, with one MP simply suggesting that they 'google it'. In between were a range of different answers that pointed the constituent to the local council or electoral office or provided a phone number or email for someone else who, they suggested, might be able to help. Overall, just over half of the emails received a response directing them to one of the main websites and only 3 per cent contained no contact information at all.

In other words, those with low expectations were wrong. Most MPs did respond, most did so quickly, and most did so usefully, even in the run-up to an election, when MPs are particularly busy.

But there's a twist. The experiment featured two versions of the email, which were allocated at random. These were identical except for the name. One was chosen to suggest that the writer was white British. The other was chosen to suggest a black African constituent – specifically Nigerian, because Commonwealth citizens have the right to vote, while black Africans living in the United Kingdom have the lowest rates of voter registration of any group. The emails were sent only to MPs in constituencies where ethnic minorities comprised at least 2.5 per cent of the population.

Similar experiments on politicians' responsiveness in other countries have found evidence of racial bias. For example, one study found that US state legislators were less responsive to African American constituents. A study in China found that someone requesting information for welfare payments was significantly less likely to receive a reply if they had a Muslim name, and in Germany, public servants receiving requests for welfare services were less responsive to ethnic minority applicants.

Britain proved no different. The black African constituent received fewer responses, and those responses were less likely to contain helpful information. The differences are small, but they form part of an overall picture. The black African constituent was less likely to receive a response, by just over 3 percentage points. This difference rose to just over 6 percentage points for

Conservative MPs. The black African constituent was also less likely to be directed to one of the main websites, by 5 percentage points. And they were twice as likely as the white British constituent to receive no contact information. Beyond response rates, the responses they received were only about half as likely to include an explicit 'welcome' to the constituency as those to the white British constituent. BAME MPs did not influence this pattern, as they were no more likely to respond to the black African constituent.

On one level, voters should be reassured by these findings. MPs will respond to them when they have an issue, and most will do so very quickly. That is more than can be said for many other public services. And in most cases the responses will be useful. But there is also cause for concern, because those in the population who are often the most disengaged from the political process, and who have little faith in their MP, are also the least likely to get help when they need it.

FURTHER READING

Experiments such as this one are common in studies of housing and employment discrimination. For example, Butler and Broockman's 'Do Politicians Racially Discriminate Against Constituents? A Field Experiment on State Legislators' (*American Journal of Political Science*, 2011) is a similar experiment in the US finding racial discrimination among state legislators. An in-depth account of the political integration of ethnic minority groups, including perceptions, engagement and values, can be found in Anthony Heath et al.'s *The Political Integration of Ethnic Minorities in Britain* (Oxford University Press, 2013). Matt Korris's 'A Year in the Life: from Member of Public to Member of Parliament' (Hansard Society, 2011) gives an insight into the work that MPs do.

—CHAPTER 14—

Turnout for what? The (mis)measurement of electoral participation

Christopher Prosser

E lectoral turnout is an important measure of democratic health: when turnout goes down, more voices are left unheard in the political process. As a key indicator of democratic health, it is important that we measure turnout accurately. However, in many countries – including Britain – we do not.

Calculating the proportion of voters who turned out seems simple: you just divide the number of votes by the number of people eligible to vote. The first number is easy. The problem lies in the second: knowing how many people were eligible to vote in the first place is much trickier. There are two valid numbers we could use: the total number of people who are legally entitled to participate in elections, whether or not they are registered to do so (the voting-eligible population, as academics call it), or the number of people who are actually registered to vote in the election (registered voters). For those interested in overall democratic participation, voting-eligible population turnout is more useful. From an electoral administration perspective, registered voter turnout might be more appropriate. In Britain, at least, which number we should use is a moot point, since we do not know either of them.

This may come as a surprise to election watchers, who will undoubtedly recall turnout being reported and widely discussed after each election. At the 2017 general election, for example, turnout was said to be 68.7 per cent. This number is arrived at by dividing the number of votes cast (32.2 million) by what is (misleadingly) described as the 'total registered electorate' (46.8 million). This second number should more accurately be described as the 'total number of entries on the electoral register'. But there are substantially more entries on the electoral register than there are people who are registered to vote. This is for two reasons.

First, although everyone is entitled to vote only once, some people (for example, university students and people who live in more than one home) are allowed to register to vote in multiple places. There are 2.3 million students in Britain and 5.2 million second-home owners. Duplicate entries therefore potentially make up as many as 16 per cent of total entries on the register, although the true proportion is likely much smaller. There is no record of who is registered more than once, so we cannot know for certain how many register entries are duplicates, but when respondents to the British Election Study Internet Panel were asked, only 23 per cent of full-time students and 2 per cent of second-home owners appear to be registered in more than one place. This still suggests about 600,000 duplicate entries on the electoral register.

The second problem is much larger. As well as legitimate duplicates, the electoral register contains a large number of inaccurate entries which arise when people move but are not deregistered at their previous address, when people die (as discussed in Chapter 38) and when mistakes are made during registration. The Electoral Commission conducts periodic reviews of the accuracy and completeness of the electoral register. In their December 2015 study, they found that the registers were 91 per cent accurate. Or, in other words, there were about 4 million entries on the electoral register that should not be there.

Once you take the numbers of duplicate and inaccurate register entries into account, we get an estimate of about 42.2 million people who are registered to vote in the UK. This means that the 2017 registered voter turnout was, we think, about 76.3 per cent, 7.6 points higher than what it was reported to be. It is obviously good news that turnout is higher than we thought, although, however you measure it, registered voter turnout in Britain dropped precipitously in the late 1990s and early 2000s and has only partially recovered since.

Registered voter turnout is also problematic because it ignores the large number of people who are eligible to vote but are unregistered. So why don't we use the voting-eligible population figure instead? Because we do not know that number either. The Electoral Commission estimated that there were about 8 million unregistered but otherwise eligible people in December 2015. Nor does the government publish any statistics that tell us what the voting-eligible population is. They do publish figures for the size of the adult population (the 'voting-age population') but this also includes many people who are ineligible to vote, such as millions of non-Commonwealth migrants who reside in Britain but lack British citizenship.

Because it is an easy number to work out, voting-age population turnout is commonly used in academic research to compare turnout between countries. This is very problematic because the number of ineligible residents varies considerably between countries and over time. Here's a simple example: did turnout go up or down at the 2015 UK election, compared to 2010? According to the officially reported turnout, it went up slightly. If we look at voting-age population turnout, it went down. We cannot say with absolute certainty which of these answers is correct but based on our best estimate of the voting-eligible population, it went up. Voting-age population turnout gives us the wrong answer because the number of ineligible residents grew more between 2010 and 2015 than the number of people voting, due, for example, to the settlement of a large number of EU migrants ineligible to vote in elections.

The problems with measuring turnout are even worse if we want to compare turnout between countries. In some places, the electoral registers are very accurate. Sweden, for example, bases its electoral registers on the Swedish population register, and the registers are thought to be close to 100 per cent accurate. Other countries have electoral registers that are even less accurate than the UK's. In the United States, for example, thanks to a well-intentioned law designed to make it harder to deregister voters, the number of inaccurate entries has grown massively in the past twenty-five years. At the current rate, there will be more names on the electoral register than there are people eligible to vote by the 2036 election. In some countries, this is already the case – in

Portugal, for example, there are nearly one million more entries on the electoral register than there are adults living there.

There has been much research published that compares turnout rates between countries, which measures turnout using either registered voter or voting-age population turnout. We know these measures are problematic, and so we should not trust the conclusions drawn from this research. Measuring turnout is difficult, but if we care about democracy, we need to do it properly.

FURTHER READING

For a detailed look at the accuracy and completeness of the British electoral registers see the Electoral Commission's 'The December 2015 electoral registers in Great Britain' report (similar reports are available for other years). For an examination of the problems with measuring turnout in the US see 'The Myth of the Vanishing Voter' by Michael McDonald and Samuel Popkin (*American Political Science Review*, 2001). For one of the few efforts to compare turnout using the voting-eligible population see Daniel Stockemer's 'Electoral Participation: How to Measure Voter Turnout?' (*Social Indicators Research*, 2016). The discussion of British data draws on a paper written with my British Election Study colleagues: 'Aggregate Turnout Is Mismeasured' by Jon Mellon et al. (2018).

CHAPTER 15

Turn over, tune out and log off: the irrelevance of campaigns

Mark Pack

Think back to the last Olympic medal ceremony you saw. Did you wait with bated breath to see who would outpace the others and snatch the gold by beating them to the top step? Of course not. Because we all know who gets which medal has been determined before the medal ceremony. A commentator who narrated the walk out to the podium as if it determines who gets the gold medal would, rightly, be dismissed as eccentric. Possibly lovable, but certainly eccentric.

Yet when it comes to British general elections nearly everyone falls foul of the same eccentric behaviour, treating the last few weeks of a parliamentary cycle – the formal general election campaign itself – as if they are what determines the election result. But much of the race has been run long before the formal campaign – and in almost every general election in the last sixty years the party that was ahead in the polls months before the formal election campaign started was the one that went on to win.

The rush of extended political coverage in newspapers, the special extra TV broadcasts, the journalists sent on tours of marginal seats in 'quirky' forms of transport, the extra generosity of financial donors, the ramping up of political party advertising campaigns, the prognostications of pundits about how today's events might be the turning point in the campaign – they are all far too late. The result is already settled.

The table below gives you the data to prove it. It lists each general election since 1960, showing the party ahead in the polls in January of that year – and then the winning party when the votes were counted.

PARTIES AHEAD AT START OF YEAR AND AT GENERAL ELECTION

ELECTION	PARTY PREDICTED TO GET THE MOST VOTES	PARTY WHICH GOT THE MOST VOTES
1964	Labour	Labour
1966	Labour	Labour
1970	Conservative	Conservative
1974 Feb	Conservative	Conservative (but Labour got most seats)
1974 Oct	n/a	Labour
1979	Conservative	Conservative
1983	Conservative	Conservative
1987	Conservative	Conservative
1992	Conservative	Conservative
1997	Labour	Labour
2001	Labour	Labour
2005	Labour	Labour
2010	Conservative	Conservative
2015	Labour	Conservative
2017	Conservative	Conservative

Source: Data taken from the opinion poll database at http://www.markpack.org.uk/opinion-polls/.

Across these fifteen elections, in thirteen cases the party ahead in January went on to win. The two exceptions are of the sort that really do fit the 'exception that proves the rule' cliché. One, in 2015, was a case when the opinion polls turned out to be way out. If you adjust polling figures from January 2015 in line with the polls' final errors then the rule still works (as it does if you make similar adjustments for the other two general elections where the polls were way out). The second exception is October 1974 where looking at the January figures is meaningless because going back to January means going back to before the *previous* general election. But even in the short interregnum between the two 1974 elections, the basic point that the party ahead well in advance went on to win still holds. Nor is January a magic month – the same strong overall pattern persists with a wrinkle or two along the way if you nudge the calendar a little this way or that.

The 2017 election was almost the perfect storm for the rule to break down: a huge switch in the popularity of party leaders during a campaign, a huge swing in voting intentions, a remarkably incompetent campaign by the incumbent. It all added up to a perfect set of excuses as to why the rule might not hold. But it still held.

Why is it the case that the sound and fury of election campaigns themselves amount to making no difference to who wins? Partly it is down to the campaign efforts of different parties mostly cancelling each other out. (If a political party would like to try out not campaigning at all so we can test this more rigorously, please do get in touch.) Partly it is due to the heavy influence of demography, class and habits on people's voting intentions, none of which change more than a smidgen during the brevity of an election campaign itself. Partly it is down to the influence of parties' reputations, which also come with years of baggage rather than being forged in the heat of the last few weeks of a campaign. Even when a single moment does shift a party's reputation – as with the Conservatives when Britain crashed out of the Exchange Rate Mechanism (ERM) in 1992 – these moments usually happen outside election campaigns because they are caused by events and decisions on a more fundamental scale than who said what at which press conference (or, these days, on Twitter).

So what should you do? Pay more attention to the past. If you wanted to understand the 2015 general election, you would have been far better off paying attention to how Labour failed to defend its economic record in 2010–11 than the latest twists of Ed Miliband's face as he came into contact with voters or bacon rolls.

Of course, in close individual seats the last few weeks of the campaign makes a difference, and for those who are putting in the sort of campaigning hours each week that make junior doctors look like part-timers, what happens in the last few weeks of their years of effort in a seat certainly does matter to them. And, as 2017 showed, it can also make a difference to the margin of victory, influencing how the predicted winner ends up governing even if it does not change who the winner is.

But for the bigger picture as to who is going to win and the name of the next Prime Minister? Pay heed to the evidence: take a look at the polls shortly after Christmastime, place a bet if you are a betting person and then put your feet up. You can safely let almost all the political news pass you by without altering your understanding of the likely election result and its causes. For if you do want to know why the result is going to be what it will be, turn off the rolling news, log out of Twitter and open a history book or two.

FURTHER READING

For an expert dissection of the impact of longer-term factors on voting behaviour over several recent British general elections see *Affluence, Austerity and Electoral Change in Britain* (Oxford University Press, 2013) by Paul Whiteley et al. The Labour Party in particular has lost a sequence of general elections due to long-term factors, and a good picture of how such issues are seen through the eyes of voters is painted in Deborah Mattinson's *Talking to a Brick Wall* (Biteback, 2010). More broadly, there is evidence that campaigns can matter in lower-profile elections and in other countries. A good review of the research on this is in 'How do campaigns matter?' by Gary C. Jacobson (*Annual Review of Political Science*, 2015).

'Politics would be a helluva good business if it weren't for the goddamned people.'

— RICHARD NIXON

CHAPTER 16

Of mousers and men: how politics colours everything we see

Robert Ford

One important, yet rarely discussed, political decision is who is to fill the post of Chief Mouser to the Cabinet Office, a position which stretches back at least to Stanley Baldwin's time in office. Incumbents often hold the role for a long time: Mrs Thatcher's second cat, Humphrey (allegedly named after a fictional civil servant with similar feline cunning), joined Downing Street in 1989 and remained in office through the rest of her term and that of her successor, John Major, finally retiring from service in 10 Downing Street during Tony Blair's first term in office. The current incumbent, Larry, is also a veteran: he took up his position in 2011.

Like all Whitehall civil servants, the Downing Street cats are resolutely apolitical, serving at the pleasure of Her Majesty's government, whichever political tribe takes the helm. But this is not how they are seen by the electorate. In an experiment run with the survey company YouGov, a representative sample of voters were shown a picture of the redoubtable Humphrey randomly varying whether he was described as Margaret Thatcher's cat or Tony Blair's cat and asked to say whether they liked or disliked him. The figure below shows how the net approval of Humphrey the cat (the share who like Humphrey minus the share who dislike him) varies depending on the partisanship of the respondents doing the rating, and the Prime Minister with whom Humphrey is associated.

NET APPROVAL OF HUMPHREY THE CAT BY PARTISANSHIP AND DESCRIPTION OF OWNER

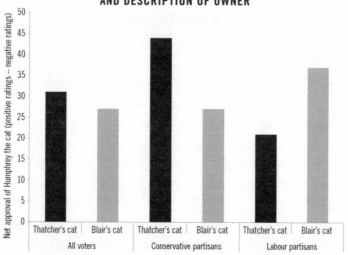

Source: YouGov poll of 2,190 voters, April 2014.

Humphrey comes out with a strongly positive net rating (unlike most of the politicians he served) and his average rating among all voters is not much affected by association with Thatcher or Blair. The views of partisan respondents, however, are strongly affected by Humphrey's perceived owner. Conservative voters show a much stronger affection for Mrs Thatcher's cat than for an identical cat associated with Mr Blair, while Labour partisans show the opposite preference. The same was true in a second experiment using pictures of the (different) cats resident in Downing Street during Gordon Brown and David Cameron's terms in office. Labour identifiers gave a cat associated with Gordon Brown a net rating of +50, but the same cat scored just +37 with Conservative partisans. Larry, Cameron's cat, scored +52 with Conservative identifiers but +40 with Labour loyalists. Nor is partisanship the only political attachment to influence views of the Chief Mouser: ideological values, views about national identity, gender and age are all associated with views of Humphrey and his successors, and these effects vary depending on the perceived owner. The public, it seems, buy into the theory that pets resemble their owners, but apply it to political outlook as well as appearance or personality.

The tale of Humphrey's politics illustrates a more serious point: our own political attachments and values tend to colour our views of anything and everything we associate with politics. Similar experiments conducted in the United States have shown that racially prejudiced Americans dislike Barack Obama's dog, which doesn't sound so harmful, but they also dislike any and every policy associated with Barack Obama, which certainly is. Racially intolerant Americans approved of Obama's reforms to expand access to health care for the young and the poor, but disapproved of identical reforms when they were associated with the President. One American late-night comedian confronted voters with this inconsistency, and found that many simply refused to believe that the health care reforms they supported were the same thing as the 'Obamacare' they rejected.

Attaching policies to politicians can thus short circuit entirely any rational consideration of their costs and benefits, replacing them with ideological and tribal loyalties. British researchers have found similar effects: voters interviewed around the time of the 1997 election tended to support policies associated with Tony Blair and Labour, but reject identical policies when they were attributed to John Major and the Conservatives, a phenomenon known as the 'halo and forked tail effect'. Partisanship also skews how voters judge responsibility: partisans are eager to give their preferred party credit for successes, and to absolve them from blame for failures. Since the EU referendum, Leave and Remain partisanship have begun similarly to colour how voters view the world, with Remain voters taking a dim view of anyone and anything associated with Leave, and vice versa (see, for example, Chapter 39).

In an idealised democracy, voters will assess the merits of policies and politicians, and then choose between them. In reality, voters often do the opposite: attached to one political tribe, their views of policies, politicians (and pets) are driven by whether these are seen as on our team or their team.

We should not be too harsh on the electorate. Politics is a complicated business, and voters are busy people. When they are presented with a difficult new problem they haven't considered before and know little about, such as education reform or banking regulation, they will naturally search for a shortcut. If the party they trust and support backs a reform, they will reason, it is probably a good idea. If the party they oppose and dislike is keen, then perhaps it is not. People use such intellectual shortcuts, known as heuristics, all the time: much of advertising is designed to exploit them. In a complicated and fast-moving world, it is hard to see how many of us could function without some shortcuts to reduce the torrent of information we face to more manageable proportions.

Yet a necessary survival strategy for voters – lean on what you do know when deciding about things you don't – poses troubling questions for the operation of a political system. How can new policies turn around the fortunes of an unpopular party, if even popular ideas become tainted by association? Should parties spend less time designing good policy, and more time building their brands and finding popular leaders? How much attention should politicians pay to the views of media and interest group elites, when such people spend most of their waking hours focused on politics, and therefore have little in common with the average voter, who rarely thinks about it at all? The next time you see a politician struggling to explain his latest ideas for solving the nation's problems, bear in mind that most of those watching are not going to give him a fair hearing including, most likely, you.

FURTHER READING

The experiment on Barack Obama's pet dog is described in Michael Tesler's 'The Spillover of Racialization into Evaluations of Bo Obama'. The broader range of experiments examining how support for policies is influenced by their association with Obama can be found in Tesler's *Post Racial or Most Racial? Race and Politics in the Obama Era* (University of Chicago Press, 2016). The experiments demonstrating that partisanship determines how voters attribute credit and blame are found in James Tilley and Sara Hobolt's 'Is the Government to Blame? An Experimental Test of How Partisanship Shapes Perceptions of Performance and Responsibility' (*Journal of Politics*, 2011), while more recent evidence on how Brexit colours how voters view the world can be found in 'Emerging Brexit Identities' by Sara Hobolt et al. (2018).

—CHAPTER 17—

Neither Arthur nor Martha: gender identities

Nicola Wildash

Gender is an essential demographic within all surveys and is fundamental to social research. Historically, most (if not all) research companies asked the question as follows:

Are you male or female?

1. Male
2. Female

It's a binary, forced choice, question. All respondents are expected to know this information, and it allows pollsters to match up this demographic to official data (from the Office for National Statistics), increasing the representativeness of their samples and the accuracy and reliability of data.

Back in 2015, YouGov were approached by the Nonbinary Inclusion Project to discuss this standard gender question. This grassroots organisation fights for the inclusion and recognition of non-binary people in law, media and everyday life, and wanted to understand how the market research industry approached the issue of gender. Discussions with this organisation inspired YouGov to explore the question of how straightforward gender actually is. To investigate, they contacted a nationally representative study of over 14,000 British adults and asked them to place themselves on a numeric scale where 0 was female and 100 was male.

While most people placed themselves at the far ends of the scale, there were many who did not – more than we had expected. Our assumption was that a small number of respondents might not identify as male or female (and place themselves along the scale) but the overall picture would be that most women would describe themselves as 100 per cent female and most men as 100 per cent male.

We firstly grouped all women who said 0 and all men who said 100 into group 1 (representing those who see their gender as 100 per cent male or female). Women who gave an answer between 1 and 5 and men who gave an answer between 95 and 99 were placed into group 2 or 'Strong'. The final group (group 3) included everyone who placed themselves anywhere else on the scale (between 6 and 94). For our initial analysis, we removed anyone who placed themselves on the opposite side of the scale to what was expected in case these answers were given by mistake, for example a man who gave an answer of 0. We also removed the 281 people (44 per cent men and 56 per cent women) who answered 'Not sure'.

The results showed that almost half of men (48 per cent) see themselves at the extreme end of the gender scale compared with only 7 per cent of women. Over two thirds of women identified strongly but not completely as a female. The majority of people identify with one gender or another, but women are less likely to state themselves as being 100 per cent female.

To investigate this difference further, YouGov repeated the experiment in other countries in Europe to see whether this pattern only applied in Britain. We contacted representative samples of over 1,000 adults in France, Germany, Denmark and Sweden. As the table shows, the pattern was mirrored among all the countries we looked at, with men more likely than women to perceive themselves as 100 per cent their gender.

PERCENTAGE OF MEN AND WOMEN IN EACH GENDER IDENTITY GROUP

GENDER IDENTITY GROUP	BRITAIN MALE	BRITAIN FEMALE	GERMANY MALE	GERMANY FEMALE	FRANCE MALE	FRANCE FEMALE	DENMARK MALE	DENMARK FEMALE	SWEDEN MALE	SWEDEN FEMALE
100% (1)	48	7	32	4	32	5	47	7	45	7
Strong (2)	32	70	36	65	32	56	32	65	28	61
Weak (3)	19	23	31	31	36	39	21	29	27	33

So what is causing this? Perhaps the scale was too difficult for some to understand or complete, but unless we are going to entertain the notion that women don't understand scales and men do, that doesn't offer an explanation for the sex differences we find.

What could be happening, though, is that men and women *perceive* the question in different ways. The question 'Where would you place yourself on the following scale?', although simple, leaves much to the eye of the beholder. Perhaps men are seeing this as a purely biological question, resulting in larger numbers of them choosing 100 per cent male as their answer. In contrast, women might be thinking of their biology combined with personality and character traits, resulting in a higher number of women placing themselves away from the extreme end of the scale.

The group of respondents who placed themselves on the opposite side of the scale to what we expected also reinforces this argument: ninety-nine men placed themselves on the female half of the scale while 181 women placed themselves on the male side. We assume that those (three men and thirty-six women) who put themselves at the furthest point on the opposite side may have answered in error. However, almost 50 per cent more women than men placed themselves on the opposite side of the scale, which could further illustrate that women were answering the question differently to men – choosing to answer in terms of personality rather than biology and revealing a sort of 'tomboy effect'.

This data may also be an illustration of modern-day masculinity. It is not illogical to argue that men are more uncomfortable with the idea that they are not 100 per cent male and therefore see the extreme value as the obvious answer to give. It is not that men are wrongly identifying themselves as male, but that they want to say they are *100 per cent* male. This also appears to be the case when comparing age groups. Older generations are less likely to place themselves away from the extreme ends of the scale (in Britain a third of 18–24-year-olds were in group 3 compared with just 15 per cent of over-sixties), supporting this idea that different people will perceive the question differently – and that gender is not so straightforward after all.

Since this research was carried out, the thinking behind gender questions has evolved, in part due to campaigning by organisations like the Nonbinary Inclusion Project. Many researchers are now moving away from a dualistic approach. For example, the Market Research Society now urges firms to avoid binary questions; the Office for National Statistics has been investigating potential alternatives for the 2021 Census; and Ipsos MORI now offer four options, including 'In another way' and 'Prefer not to say'. Put simply, as public understandings of gender continue to evolve, the categories researchers use will do so as well.

FURTHER READING

For work on gender and sexuality generally see Judith Butler's book *Undoing Gender* (Routledge, 2004). For thoughts on modern masculinities and femininities see *Gender, Culture and Society: Contemporary Femininities and Masculinities* by Máirtin Mac an Ghaill and Chris Haywood (Palgrave Macmillan, 2007) or 'Re-examining Masculinity, Femininity, and Gender Identity Scales' by Kay M. Palan, Charles S. Areni and Pamela Kiecker (*Marketing Letters*, 1999). For sociological approaches to understanding how and why social work is arranged around gender distinctions see Mary Holmes's book *What is Gender? Sociological Approaches* (Sage, 2007). The MRS guidance notes on collection data on sex and gender were published in January 2016.

CHAPTER 18

Too scared to switch: why voters' emotions matter

Markus Wagner

E motions have a bad name in politics. Voters who are seen as emotional are said to be swayed by appeals to their insecurities and prejudices, easily manipulated and just one step away from an uncontrollable mob. The ideal voter is often portrayed as one who thinks objectively and rationally about parties and policies, and takes their electoral decisions with due care and attention.

But this dichotomy between a cool, objective voter and an instinctive, emotional voter is a false one. We cannot divide our thinking into rational on the one hand and emotional on the other. Rather, emotions are always part of how we respond to the world around us.

Recent research in political psychology has identified two ways of thinking about emotions. The first is to distinguish positive from negative emotions. What we think about objects, events and people can make us experience positive feelings such as hope and enthusiasm: one example is how many Americans saw Barack

Obama's candidacy in 2008 and some no doubt saw Donald Trump's campaign in 2016. Sometimes, however, we experience negative feelings such as disgust, anger or fear: this is how some people react to gay marriage, immigration or economic insecurity. One important finding of this research is that negative emotions can make us more rational: because we are uncertain and anxious, we look for new information, try to find out more about the threat we perceive, and take more careful decisions about how to respond to it. Negative emotions make us less likely to act quickly and without caution; it's when we are feeling enthusiastic that we may be over-confident about the quality of our choices.

The second way of thinking about emotions is to look at each reaction as a distinct emotion. Anger is not the same as fear, which is not the same as disgust. A good example is the financial and economic crisis and recession of the late 2000s. The 2010 survey of the British Election Study (BES) included questions about voters' emotional reactions to the recession. Respondents could choose up to four emotions from a list of eight: angry, happy, disgusted, hopeful, uneasy, confident, afraid and proud.

Negative emotions predominated. The emotion selected most often was 'uneasy' (62 per cent of respondents), followed by 'angry' (50 per cent), 'disgusted' (39 per cent) and 'afraid' (31 per cent). But there is only limited overlap between these negative emotions: for instance, only 44 per cent of those who selected 'angry' also selected 'afraid'. Distinct emotional responses to the crisis were found. While the actions of banks and governments that led to the worst recession in generations made many voters angry, other voters, scared that the economic problems would lead them to lose their jobs and their livelihood, were more afraid than angry.

(Perhaps understandably, fewer than 12 per cent of participants chose one or more positive emotions.) These kinds of differentiated emotions are important whenever people react to political events. For instance, a survey in 2015 found that 26 per cent of voters felt 'hopeful' when thinking about Britain's EU membership, but 18 per cent felt 'angry' and 16 per cent 'afraid'.

Blame plays an important part in determining these negative emotional reactions. Anger is a natural response if we hold someone responsible for a threatening event. A tree in your garden felled by a neighbour might make you angry, a tree felled by a storm less so. The influence of blame is especially strong if we think that the person or organisation responsible should have looked out for us and cared about our welfare instead of causing damage.

The financial crisis provides an illustration of this as well. The BES asked participants to identify who, if anyone, they held responsible for the crisis: the UK government, the EU, or international actors, for instance banks or the US government. Those who could identify a responsible actor were angrier than those who could not, so it is important whether or not we assign blame. Moreover, those who saw the UK government or the EU as responsible were angrier than those who blamed the banks or the US government. These are institutions that we help to elect and who are responsible for our welfare, so anger is perhaps an understandable response.

Different emotions also encourage different behaviours. Anger makes us want to remove the source of harm and leads us to engage in risk-seeking behaviour. This is what evolutionary psychologists call the 'approach system': angry people seek out the source of their anger, even at risk to themselves. But fear makes us pursue risk-averse behaviour and increases our vigilance. This is the 'avoidance system': people who are afraid try to escape the source of their fear.

Again, the financial crisis gives a good example. The BES surveys, which measured voting behaviour in 2005 and 2010 as well as emotional reactions, show that loyalty to Labour differed depending on whether respondents were angry or afraid about the recession. Those who voted Labour in 2005 and who were angry about the crisis were 14 per cent less likely to vote Labour again in 2010 than those who were not. When explaining electoral decisions, 14 per cent is a big effect for a single factor. In contrast, fear had no effect: previous Labour voters who were afraid about the crisis were not less likely to vote Labour again than those voters who were not. This fits with what we know about the impact of emotions: anger encourages people to take action against the source of their anger, so angry voters took out their anger on Labour by switching support. Fearful voters did not take action in the same way. These two emotions were both reasonable feelings to have about the dramatic and confusing events of 2007 and after, but they had very different effects on the decisions taken by the voters who felt them. Similar effects hold for Brexit as well: fearful voters were more supportive of renegotiating the terms of membership, whereas angry ones were more willing to just go ahead and leave the EU.

Our emotional reactions to events play a complex role in how we think about politics and how we take voting decisions. Having emotions does not turn voters into irrational, easily manipulated individuals. Emotions are unavoidable, and so we should not distinguish between rational, objective and thus 'good' decision-making and emotional, affect-driven and thus 'bad' decision-making.

FURTHER READING

For the positive-negative emotions approach see, for example, *Affective Intelligence and Political Judgment* by George E. Marcus et al. (University of Chicago Press, 2000); for the distinct emotions approach see, for example, Jennifer S. Lerner and Dacher Keltner's 'Fear, Anger, and Risk' (*Journal of Personality and Social Psychology*, 2001). The findings on the financial crisis are published in Markus Wagner, 'Fear and Anger in Great Britain: Blame Assignment and Emotional Reactions to the Financial Crisis' (*Political Behavior*, 2014). The findings on Brexit are detailed in Sofia Vasilopoulou and Markus Wagner, 'Fear, anger and enthusiasm about the European Union: Effects of emotional reactions on public preferences towards European integration' (*European Union Politics*, 2017).

CHAPTER 19

What's in a name: ballot order effects

Galina Borisyuk

Those wishing to seek elected office in the UK may want to change their surname. Other things being equal, it is better to be Brown not Smith. But Brown and Smith are each better than Borisyuk – not that I'm thinking of standing.

If you study the distribution of votes cast in local council wards where voters are selecting more than a single councillor, you will notice a high level of unused votes. Say 1,000 electors each have three votes the total number of votes cast could be 3,000; but it often isn't. Some unused votes arise because parties fail to field enough candidates for the number of seats available; three seats but only two candidates, for example. In such cases the partisan electors might baulk at the idea of using their spare vote for a rival party and would not use their full quota. But even in those elections where the parties field full slates of candidates you still find some voters (about one in fifteen in London and as high as one in nine in other larger cities) who do not take full advantage of all the votes available to them.

Maybe these unused votes arise because people did not understand the voting system. Since most people read text (in this case a ballot paper) from left to right and from top to bottom, you might think that candidates located towards the top of the ballot paper should do better than those located towards the bottom. After examining tens of thousands of local ballots one study discovered that a candidate's finishing position within a party slate depends upon the position on the ballot paper as a whole, his or her alphabetic rank within the party slate, and whether they were an incumbent seeking re-election or challenging an incumbent. To be fair, incumbency mattered more than alphabetic order but surnames were associated with vote differences. The alphabetic advantage between the first and last placed candidates on the ballot paper was real, and increased along with the number of available seats and the number of competitors.

Alphabetic bias is not restricted to these relatively complex ballots. It appears to extend to very simple electoral contests. Alphabetic effects have been found even in single-member local council seats. In the simplest possible electoral situation – that is, two candidates contesting one seat – there is a mean difference of eleven votes (or 0.6 percentage points) between the person placed second and bottom of the ballot paper compared to the name encountered first on the ballot paper. As the number of candidates increases so the difference in vote between first and last in the alphabetic order also grows.

What are the consequences of this for representative government? A separate study examined over 600,000 candidate names that appeared on local council election ballots from the early '70s onwards. They were divided into ten equal categories according to surname. It turns out that the distribution among those elected is clustered towards the first three surname categories (A'Beckett to Flello in this case). The elected are under-represented in the bottom five categories (surnames running from Kennedy to Zygadllo).

This evidence suggests that approximately 2,050 councillors elected between 1973 and 2012 owe their election to ballot position alone. This might not seem like a large number over a long period although for the 2,050 that were not elected because their name happened to be further down the ballot paper it must hurt.

But there was something else in the data. The relationship between surname and electoral support is not entirely linear. The advantage for those at the very top of the ballot was not as high as expected. One possibility was an association between alphabetic order and ethnicity. Non-European names, for example, are particularly abundant in the first surname category. In order to examine this ethnic dimension computer software was used to allocate surnames into three types: British (Anglo-Saxon, Celtic), other European and non-European. It became clear that in addition to relative ballot position a candidate's vote was also being affected – positively or negatively – by perceived ethnic origin.

There are two ways of investigating this issue further. First, in the case of wards that elect multiple councillors comparisons can be made among candidates standing for the same party. Other things being equal, over this forty-year period candidates with British surnames perform best while non-European candidates performed worst. Between 1,422 and 7,150 seats could have been won by a different person had the names on the ballot papers been configured differently.

Second, the analysis of 70,000 single-member seats considered the patterns of candidate recruitment, or ethnic transition, across electoral cycles. This showed that party vote is adversely affected when British candidates are replaced by those with European and non-European surnames while the opposite pattern of succession is associated with a boost in vote. The effect of this? Up to 5,167 of these single-member seats (7 per cent of the total) were won/lost by parties by margins that might be explained by such ethnic transitions.

What is to be done?

We could do nothing, of course, and allow parties to seek out and recruit candidates with appropriate surnames in a frantic 'name race'. Political careerists should download the deed poll forms immediately. Another solution is to follow practice elsewhere. Australia and the United States are two countries where ballot order is randomised. Vancouver introduced randomised ballots in 2018. This would be fairly cheap to implement, although it makes hand-counting of ballots more complicated. A third approach might be to reform local elections and abolish the practice of multiple seats. Some voters are clearly perplexed by a complex ballot but imagine how perplexed these voters are by other voting systems now widely employed across the UK.

None of these solutions address the issue of name discrimination, however. Local parties are trying hard to recruit candidates from under-represented groups. But we should acknowledge that currently there are some voters who are still reluctant to support candidates with 'unusual' surnames.

FURTHER READING

For an examination about unused votes the best source is 'Unused votes in English Local Government Elections: Effects and Explanations' by Colin Rallings et al. (*Journal of Elections, Public Opinion and Parties*, 2009), while a more detailed analysis about the electoral effects of ballot ordering can be found in 'Ballot Order Positional Effects in British Local Elections, 1973–2011' by Richard Webber et al. (*Parliamentary Affairs*, 2014). The extent of name discrimination is investigated in 'Candidate Ethnic Origins and Voter Preferences: Examining Name Discrimination in Local Elections in Britain' by Michael Thrasher et al. (*British Journal of Political Science*, 2017).

CHAPTER 20

Racism at the ballot box: ethnic minority candidates

Stephen Fisher

B ritain's ethnic minorities are underrepresented. Just 8 per cent of MPs are from a visible ethnic minority background, compared with 13 per cent of the population according to the 2011 Census. Although the first ethnic minority MP was elected in 1841, there were none in the fifty years from 1929 to 1979.

Things have improved a lot since then, but initially only slowly. Hard-fought internal battles preceded the election of Labour's first ethnic minority MPs in 1987. It was not until 2001 that the number of ethnic minority Labour MPs reached double figures. The Conservatives never had more than two visible minority MPs at a time until eleven were elected in 2010. The total number of ethnic minority MPs took further leaps from twenty-seven in 2010 to forty-one in 2015 and fifty-two in 2017 (nineteen Conservative, thirty-two Labour and one Liberal Democrat).

There has been a corresponding rise in the number of ethnic minority candidates since the 1970s. By 2001, the number for the

Conservatives, Labour and Liberals combined was sixty-six, then 113 in 2005, 138 in 2010, and 162 in 2015. That figure fell slightly to 147 in 2017, although across all parties there were at least 261 ethnic minority candidates in 2017, up from an estimated 230 in 2015.

More ethnic minorities are willing to stand, parties are more willing to nominate them and, crucially for representation, place them in winnable and even safe seats. Is this because voters are increasingly accepting of non-white politicians?

Surveys have shown a decline in the numbers of people admitting to racial prejudice – so if they are telling the truth we should expect people to vote in a less racist way than in the past. One way to test this is to examine whether parties suffer a drop in support when they field an ethnic minority candidate. Studies of this kind in the 1980s found mixed results, in part because the low number of ethnic minority candidates standing made it hard to separate out a common pattern from individual seat idiosyncrasies. However, in every election since 1992, when either of the two main parties have switched from a white to an ethnic minority candidate in seats where there are relatively few ethnic minority residents they have suffered an average electoral penalty of 2 to 3 percentage points. There is no such discrepancy in the seats with the most ethnic minority voters.

This pattern suggests (some) white voters continue to prefer voting for white candidates, and also that (some) ethnic minorities may discriminate in favour of other minorities. Constituency results, however, are not enough to confirm this because they cannot show how individual votes depend on the ethnicity of candidates after accounting for other factors affecting vote choices. Also, constituency analysis is vulnerable to what is known as the 'ecological fallacy', where we try to infer the behaviour of individuals based on differences in average behaviour across areas with different social characteristics. We might well assume that if areas with large ethnic minority populations behave more favourably towards ethnic minority candidates, this is the result of ethnic minority voters being more likely to vote for those candidates, but we don't know this. It may instead be that white voters in such areas are less racist.

One way of getting around this is to survey individual voters. Not to ask them whether they are happy to vote for minority candidates, but to see whether their vote choices are correlated with candidate ethnicity after controlling for other factors. To be able to identify small but politically important differences in probabilities we need a large sample covering most constituencies with minority candidates. For ethnic minority voters, such a survey is only available for the 2010 general election.

When you analyse this data you find that ethnic minority candidates suffered an average electoral penalty of about 4 points at the hands of white voters.

But not all ethnic minority candidates are equally discriminated against – and not all white voters engage in racial discrimination at the ballot box. Muslim candidates were particularly discriminated against, by the three-quarters of white voters who expressed negative feelings about immigration. This ballot-box Islamophobia accounts for just over half of the overall ethnic electoral penalty. Whereas non-Muslim minority candidates appear to suffer an average penalty of 2 points, that for Muslims is as much as 8 percentage points.

And while on average white voters favour white candidates, in general, ethnic minority voters do not favour ethnic minority candidates. The exception is a clear co-ethnic effect for voters from a Pakistani background, who favoured candidates from the same background. This is not a process of Muslim voters for Muslim candidates, but something specific to the Pakistani community (and perhaps the Bangladeshi community too, although there were too few Bangladeshi candidates to be sure) and often linked to kinship networks.

Such community mobilisation is controversial among second and third generation Pakistanis and may now be in decline. There was no sign of Indian heritage voters disproportionately supporting Indian heritage candidates, or black voters favouring black candidates (either generally or considering black African and black Caribbean heritage groups separately).

Given that most ethnic minorities want more ethnic minority MPs elected and have a shared experience of discrimination, the relative lack of co-minority voting is perhaps surprising. The main explanation lies in the strength of the Labour Party among minorities. Since Labour are seen as the best party to defend minority interests, minorities tend not to abandon white Labour candidates to vote for a non-white candidate from another party, even if that candidate is from the voter's own ethnic group.

As a result of all this, constituencies with relatively large ethnic minority populations tend to vote Labour, and ethnic minority Labour candidates do relatively well in them. Taking advantage of this situation, Labour have increased minority representation by placing ethnic minority candidates in ethnic minority seats with little or no cost in votes. By contrast, in seeking to modernise and diversify his party, David Cameron's only choice was to place ethnic minority candidates in overwhelmingly white areas and suffer the electoral penalty because (some) white voters, and not just Conservatives, still prefer their MPs to be white.

It is a puzzle as to why studies have not shown a decline in the ethnic electoral penalty since the 1980s, given the decline in racism in general. There is an old quip that gender equality means female MPs should be just as bad as the male ones. Perhaps the average quality of ethnic minority candidates has gone down as parties have been more willing to accept them, and so the ethnic penalty is not balanced out by the better quality of ethnic minority candidates in the way it used to be. We shall never know, and there are other possible explanations. But it is clear that racial discrimination remains a problem at the ballot box as in other walks of life.

FURTHER READING

For a discussion of the decline in racism internationally (among many other interesting things) see Steven Pinker's *The Better Angels of Our Nature* (Penguin, 2012). The analyses of constituency results referred to above come from the appendices by John Curtice and others in the so-called Nuffield election study series, of which the latest is Philip Cowley and Dennis Kavanagh's *The British General Election of 2017* (Palgrave Macmillan, 2018). The survey data analysis referred to is from 'Candidate Ethnicity and Vote Choice in Britain' (*British Journal of Political Science*, 2015) by Stephen D. Fisher et al.

—CHAPTER 21—

Not total recall: why people lie about voting

Paul Whiteley

I t is quite a tricky problem to find out if people are telling the truth when they respond to surveys. One of the few opportunities to investigate this arises at election times, using the official records kept by local authorities to make sure that if an election is challenged they have a record of who actually voted. These records do not show *how* anyone voted, just whether or not they did, but they allow us to compare the records with people's claims about what they did on polling day.

For example, the 2010 British Election Study (BES) carried out checks on 3,515 respondents who took part in their survey. The table below compares claims of voting with actual voting for those survey respondents and shows that significant numbers of people gave misleading answers. The left-hand column shows the respondent's validated vote obtained from the polling records after the election. The next two columns report the respondent's self-identified turnout in the post-election wave of the survey. Thus 55.6 per cent of all respondents claimed they had voted in person when questioned in the survey, and the validation exercise confirmed they were telling the truth. Another 10.7 per cent of respondents correctly reported voting by post or by proxy. Combining these two categories, we find just over 66 per cent of people correctly reported voting, which is approximately the same as the recorded turnout in the election.

REPORTED VOTE AND ACTUAL VOTING IN THE 2010 GENERAL ELECTION

VALIDATED VOTE	SELF-REPORTED VOTE		
	VOTED (%)	DID NOT VOTE (%)	TOTAL (%)
Voted in person	55.6	1.7	57.3
Postal/proxy vote	10.7	0.2	11.0
Not eligible to vote	0.3	0.4	0.7
Eligible but did not vote	6.3	13.6	19.9
Not on the register	5.0	6.2	11.2
TOTAL	77.8	22.2	100.0

Source: British Election Study 2010.

The interesting section of the table relates to those who either did not remember what they did on election day or provided incorrect answers. Firstly, some respondents said they voted but either could not, because they weren't on the electoral register, or did not, because the register confirmed they never cast a ballot. Some 5.3 per cent of all respondents claimed to have voted when they were actually ineligible (0.3 per cent) or not on the register (5.0 per cent), and a further 6.3 per cent claimed to have voted, and were on the register, but never marked a ballot. Combining these categories, 11.6 per cent of survey respondents incorrectly claimed to have participated in the election. At the time of the 2010 general election this equated to about 5.3 million people, so it is a significant group.

People also make mistakes in the opposite direction, claiming not to have voted when in fact they did: 1.7 per cent of respondents in the survey forgot that they had voted in person and a further 0.2 per cent forgot that they had voted by post or by proxy. But people are more likely to report false positives – claiming to vote when they did not – than false negatives – forgetting they cast a ballot. And this is an enduring problem: self-reported turnout has been consistently higher than actual turnout, and by a fairly stable difference of about 10 percentage points, going back to the first British Election Study in 1964.

The standard explanation for this is that voting is seen as a desirable thing to do by most people, and so non-voters are tempted to claim they voted in order to conform to this social norm. Yet plenty of people are happy to disregard this social norm: 13.6 per cent of interviewees declared truthfully that they did not vote, and another 6.2 per cent correctly declared they were not registered to vote. Add these groups together, and we find that one in five citizens is quite happy to ignore the social norm sanctioning abstention. Young people, who have a weaker sense that voting is something expected of a good citizen, were particularly likely to do this. So while some over-reporting is likely to reflect a desire to conform to social norms, this is unlikely to tell the whole story.

One of the other questions in the BES survey in 2010 asked respondents to estimate how likely they were to vote in the approaching general election. Responses were scored along a scale where zero meant 'very unlikely' and ten meant 'very likely'. When this is analysed in comparison with records of voting, it turns out that high scores on this scale were associated with incorrectly claiming to have voted after the election. In other words, if individuals did not expect to vote to begin with, they were quite content to admit to an interviewer that they had not voted. But if they really wanted to vote and subsequently, for whatever reason, failed to do so, they were more likely to mislead the interviewers.

The psychologist Dan Ariely claims that behaviour like this is driven by two opposing motivations – what he calls 'fudge factor theory'. One of these motivations is to see ourselves as honest and honourable people. The other is to take advantage of opportunities to cheat and free ride on the efforts of other people. His experimental work shows that most individuals will take advantage of opportunities to cheat a little bit, if they can. But they will not do this to the point of having to admit to themselves that they are dishonest and unprincipled. In other words most people cheat a little bit, but only a few cheat a lot because the latter is incompatible with a good self-image.

This may be what drives the misleading answers given to interviewers. It is the result of 'cognitive dissonance' between the desire to vote on the one hand and social norms about voting on the other. Most people will recognise the social desirability norm, but the effect of this on their answers to interviewers depends on whether voting is important to them personally. People who think that their own electoral participation is not that important may well recognise that voting is seen as socially desirable, but they are less embarrassed to admit failing to meet this social standard because it is not personally important to them.

But the psychology is different for those who really wanted to vote before the election and failed to do so. They face a strong internal conflict: voting is something they regard as socially desirable and personally important, yet they failed to act in accordance with these motives. One way of dealing with this dissonance is to mislead interviewers. Another is to mislead themselves, since many respondents may not be intentionally lying but rather end up convincing themselves that they voted even when they did not.

Memories are notoriously faulty, and people often edit their recollections to suit their present self-image. However, only those who really value something go to such trouble, so when we try to assess whether respondents are giving 'socially desirable' responses in surveys, we have to know how important the particular topic is to respondents if we are to make sense of their answers. People only mislead when it matters.

FURTHER READING

The social desirability bias for voting is discussed in David E. Campbell's *Why We Vote* (Princeton University Press, 2006). Fudge factor theory is explained in Dan Ariely's *The (Honest) Truth About Dishonesty* (HarperCollins, 2012). The low levels of civic duty among young people are explored in *Affluence, Austerity and Electoral Change in Britain* by Paul Whiteley et al. (Cambridge University Press, 2013). Some of the interesting ways in which memory can deceive and people end up 'rewriting' history are discussed in Daniel Kahneman's *Thinking, Fast and Slow* (Allen Lane, 2011).

—CHAPTER 22—

Youthquake? The mystery of the missing young voters

Stuart Fox

Why have young people stopped voting in droves? That, at least, was the dominant question for those studying the way young people engaged with politics in Britain before 2017. So-called millennials, who came of age politically at the turn of the millennium, voted in numbers well below those of their parents and grandparents at the same age. In 2015, for example, the British Election Study found that around 57 per cent of millennials reported voting, compared with an average of 79 per cent of older generations. When many millennials first voted in 2005, around 49 per cent cast a ballot, compared with an average of 74 per cent of their elders. The equivalent figures for the '90s generation in 1997 were 64 per cent and 82 per cent; for the '80s generation in 1987, 71 per cent and 82 per cent; and for the '60s/'70s generation in 1974, 80 per cent and 89 per cent.

The conventional explanation was that young people cared about the issues of the day but felt excluded from traditional party politics. They were not less interested in politics than their elders but alienated from it. This claim is repeatedly invoked by those promoting policies such as lowering the voting age to increase youth turnout, and challenging it has become controversial and likely to be dismissed as blaming the young for the failures of the political elite.

The 2017 general election seemed to provide proof of this view of the world, with young people brought spectacularly back to the fold by Jeremy Corbyn's leadership of the Labour Party, his methods of campaigning, and policies such as the abolition of tuition fees. This allegedly drove young people back to the polling stations and denied the Conservative Party their majority in the House of Commons, in what on election night became known as a 'youthquake'.

There is little question that young voters overwhelmingly supported Labour in 2017 – but there are serious doubts about the existence of a 'youthquake' or that this marks a reversal of decades of low turnout among politically alienated young people.

Discounting the more ridiculous 'evidence' (such as photographs of young people standing outside polling stations on election night, or a claim of 72 per cent youth turnout tweeted by Labour MP David Lammy based on data that did not exist), the initial estimates of turnout that spawned the 'youthquake' claim were based on online polls. Estimates of the change in turnout for 18–24-year-olds (or 18–29s) between 2015 and 2017 ranged from 12 points in an exit poll conducted by NME to 21 points in a report by the Intergenerational Foundation (see the table below).

Online polls are, however, quite poor for estimating turnout because their samples are biased towards people who are interested in politics (and so more likely to vote), and because survey respondents have a well-established tendency to lie about voting (as discussed in the previous chapter).

More reliable estimates can be obtained from surveys that collect their data face-to-face and are better at recruiting representative samples. Three such surveys have showed that claims of a dramatic surge in youth turnout were misguided: the British Social Attitudes survey, Understanding Society and the British Election Study. The last is particularly important because it matches its respondents to the electoral register, making it the only survey that can check whether voters who say they voted actually did so. These surveys do not produce a consistent estimate of the change in youth turnout – ranging from negligible change to 8 points – but they are clear that there was nothing indicative of a 'youthquake'.

TURNOUT FOR YOUNG VOTERS IN 2017 (%)

SURVEY	ESTIMATED TURNOUT	ESTIMATED CHANGE 2015 TO 2017
Intergenerational Foundation	64	21
Essex Continuous Monitoring Survey	61*	19
Ipsos MORI	54	16
NME	53	12
Understanding Society	66	8
British Social Attitudes	61	6
British Election Study	43	Negligible

Note: * Estimate of turnout for under-thirties rather than 18–24-year-olds.

There is no evidence that 2017 saw a change in the political engagement or alienation of young people either. Claims that young

people are a politically alienated generation have long suffered
from an impoverished understanding of 'political alienation' –
a phrase that many use but few bother to define. The American
political scientist Ada Finifter distinguished three types of political alienation: i) powerlessness (feeling unable to influence the
political process); ii) normlessness (feeling that the rules governing fair political interaction are not being respected); and iii)
meaninglessness (a lack of confidence that one can find meaning
in politics because of a lack of understanding).

When we measure these traits in millennials, alongside their
political interest, we find that they are characterised by an unusually low level of interest in politics *and* unusually low levels of
political alienation. For example, even after accounting for the
influence of their stage in the life cycle and short-term events
that might affect how people feel about the political process, data
from the British Social Attitudes survey between 1983 and 2012
showed that millennials were typically 8 percentage points more
likely to have little or no interest in politics than older generations. At the same time, they were 9 points less likely to feel that
politicians did not listen to them (powerlessness), and 6 points
less likely to feel that politicians could not be trusted (normlessness). The only form of alienation for which they were worse off
was meaninglessness: millennials were 6 points more likely to feel
that politics was too complicated to understand.

These trends did not change after the 2017 election: a YouGov
survey after polling day showed that millennials were less likely
than their elders to agree that politicians could not be trusted or
that politicians did not care what they thought and less likely to
feel they could understand politics. The British Election Study,

meanwhile, showed that 17 per cent of millennials had no interest at all in politics, compared with 10 per cent of the wider electorate.

This all matters not just because the conventional view of potentially alienated youth or claims of a 'youthquake' are both wrong but because they are also potentially harmful. They not only incorrectly imply that there is no longer a need to worry about low youth turnout but also provide another excuse to overlook the key driver behind that trend: their declining interest in politics.

FURTHER READING

Examples of research arguing that the millennials are politically alienated include *Young People and Politics in the UK: Apathy or Alienation?* by David Marsh and colleagues (Palgrave Macmillan, 2007). Claims of a 'youthquake' can be found in Matt Henn and James Sloam's book *Youthquake 2017: The Rise of Young Cosmopolitans in Britain* (Palgrave Macmillan, 2019) and 'Why 2017 may have witnessed a Youthquake after all' by Will Jennings and Patrick Sturgis (LSE British Politics and Policy, 2018). Challenges to the 'youthquake' can be found in 'The Myth of the 2017 Youthquake Election' and 'Youthquake – a reply to our critics', both available on the British Election Study website. The definition and dimensions of political alienation can be found in Ada Finifter's 'Dimensions of Political Alienation' (*American Political Science Review*, 1970).

CHAPTER 23

Shamed into voting: how our nearest and dearest motivate us to turn out

Eline de Rooij

One of the things that puzzles political scientists is the fact that people vote. Researchers find this puzzling not because of the much-debated increase in political cynicism, but because they think voting is fundamentally irrational. Since it is very unlikely that any individual's vote will be decisive in determining the outcome of an election, each voter should realise that the outcome, for good or ill, is unlikely to be decided by their choice. They will benefit – or suffer – from the outcome whether they vote or not. So why do so many of them bother? In the last British general election in 2017, 69 per cent of registered voters voted and, although turnout at local elections tends to be lower, an average of four out of ten voters continue to cast their ballot.

One long-standing answer to this question has been that citizens perceive voting as their civic duty. We might vote not because we think we can actually affect the outcome, but because we feel we ought to. That is, we are complying with a widely accepted social norm. We live in a democracy and that requires that people vote. But do individuals comply with such a norm because it makes them feel good about themselves (what is called 'intrinsic motivation') or because they feel good as a result of showing others that they are being 'good citizens' ('extrinsic motivation')?

One type of research that tests this uses field experiments, in which voter lists are used to randomly allocate registered voters into a treatment or a control group, akin to those used in medical trials. When properly done, randomisation ensures that at the start of the experiment there are no systematic differences between the two groups. Any subsequent intervention (or 'treatment'), such as contacting those in the treatment group and encouraging them to vote, can then be fully credited with causing any differences between the treatment and control groups in voter turnout rates after the election.

One of the best-known field experimental studies conducted in the United States suggests that the extrinsic motivation to comply with the norm of voting is much stronger than the intrinsic motivation. In other words, people vote because they worry about others' opinion of them. Alan Gerber and his colleagues found that individuals who received a piece of direct mail that simply appealed to their sense of civic duty were 1.8 percentage points more likely to turn out to vote than individuals who did not. So appeals to the individual conscience mattered, but only a little. Other individuals who received a piece of direct mail that, in addition, included their recent turnout history together with that of their household members and neighbours and noted that updated information would be sent to everyone in the neighbourhood after the election, were as much as 8.1 percentage points more likely to turn out to vote.

A reminder that your neighbours can find out you stayed home on polling day acted as a more powerful spur to casting a ballot.

Another American study showed that pointing out individuals' own voting records in recent elections motivated them to a greater extent to vote than informing them of the overall voting rate in their community. This implies that social norms have their strongest effect when we feel that others may be judging us as individuals, rather than when they may be judging the community we belong to.

In our day-to-day lives, this feeling of being monitored might be greatest within the confines of our own households. Who can apply social pressure more effectively than our own family members? Thus, some studies have looked at what are called the 'spillover' effects of these experiments. The idea is simple: if social pressure influences one individual in a household, that pressure should spill over to others in the same household. One study in the US found that a doorstep canvassing campaign targeted at individuals living in two-voter households also had a substantial impact on the turnout of the household member who was not canvassed: 60 per cent of the effect of the campaign was passed on to the second household member. Evidence from a study conducted during the Police and Crime Commissioner elections in 2012 suggests that spillover also occurs within households in the UK. The study of the West Midlands contest showed that the effect of a phone call encouraging individuals to vote was fully passed on to household members. A personal reminder to a voter worked even better at motivating their partner and children when household members supported different political parties, and better still if the tone of the message was clearly partisan.

We don't know what goes on at the proverbial kitchen table that makes us more likely to vote when our partner does, but evidence from the UK study suggests that talking, rather than simply observing others voting, is key. Still, in talking, do our partners exert social pressure? Do they ignite our partisan flame? Do they remind us when and where to vote if we have forgotten amidst the many demands of our daily lives? Or, do they simply offer us a ride to the polling station when we are too lazy to go? Another study, also relying on UK data, indicates that individuals express a stronger vote intention when there is a norm to vote in their household. Together these studies suggest that although we might not know exactly what is going on, being made aware of relevant others in our lives – particularly if they have a strong sense of civic duty – monitoring our voting behaviour increases our chances of getting to the polling station on election day.

FURTHER READING

The best-known field experiment is 'Social Pressure and Voter Turnout: Evidence from a Large-scale Field Experiment' by Alan S. Gerber et al. (*American Political Science Review*, 2008) but see also 'Social Pressure, Descriptive Norms, and Voter Mobilization' by Costas Panagopolous et al. (*Political Behavior*, 2014). A brief review is 'Field Experiments on Political Behavior and Collective Action' by Eline de Rooij et al. (*Annual Review of Political Science*, 2009). Spillover effects are examined in David W. Nickerson's 'Is Voting Contagious? Evidence from Two Field Experiments' (*American Political Science Review*, 2008). The UK evidence can be found in Florian Foos and Eline de Rooij's 'All in the Family: Partisan Disagreement and Electoral Mobilization in Intimate Networks—A Spillover Experiment' (*American Journal of Political Science*, 2017) and Edward Fieldhouse and David Cutts's 'Shared Partisanship, Household Norms and Turnout: Testing a Relational Theory of Electoral Participation' (*British Journal of Political Science*, 2018).

—CHAPTER 24—

All swingers now? The rise and rise of the British swing voter

Jonathan Mellon

For decades political parties have competed furiously for one of the great prizes of British politics: the affections of the swing voter. It wasn't that long ago that there were relatively few political swingers: until the 1990s, fewer than a quarter of voters would switch parties from one election to the next.

Yet that once relatively rare breed is becoming increasingly common, which means party campaigners are going to have to come up with new tactical thinking. The British Election Study survey panels, conducted episodically over the last fifty years, are unique in that they are able to track the same voters from one election to the next, unlike more conventional opinion polls that only look at a snapshot of voters at a given time. Using these studies, you can identify the percentage of voters who switch their vote from one party to another between each pair of elections since 1966 when such data was first collected.

In 1966 only around 13 per cent of voters had changed their minds since the previous election in 1964. Since then, the proportion of swingers has been steadily increasing, and by 2015, 43 per cent of voters backed a different party to the one they supported in 2010. The increase in swing voters is pretty consistent. The three exceptions are between February and October 1974, when the short eight-month gap between elections left little time for switching to take place; between 1997 and 2001, when the electoral dominance of New Labour under Tony Blair held back the tide for a time; and finally in 2017, which still saw 33 per cent of voters switch parties (the second highest figure on record) despite only two years having elapsed since the previous vote. The 2017 election also saw the highest recorded level of direct switching between Labour and the Conservatives.

A lot of vote shifting can go on even between elections where the overall result remains stable. In 2001, for example, more people switched votes than in any election before 1997, with a surprising level of turmoil beneath the surface stability. While these largely cancelled out on that occasion, it set the stage for more dramatic changes in the parties' votes later on.

So British voters now seem more likely than ever to jump from party to party. But who exactly are these swingers? Are they disillusioned former party loyalists? Or have British voters simply stopped getting into a serious relationship with the parties in the first place? We can get some insight into this using data from the yearly British Social Attitudes Survey, looking at the number of respondents who say that they do not identify with any of the political parties (party identifiers tend to switch much less often) when they are asked 'Generally speaking, do you think of yourself as a supporter of any one political party?' and then 'Do you think of yourself as a little closer to one political party than to the others?' if they say no to the first question. The graph below combines data from 1984 to 2013. Each line represents people who first were eligible to vote under a different government. Higher lines mean that there are more people who identify with a political party. So, for instance, voters who came of age before 1964 started with very high levels of identification (77 per cent), which have stayed mostly constant ever since. Most of the lines on the graph fell in the 2000s, which shows that almost all generations fell out of love with the parties during the New Labour years, although there has been a small recovery since then.

PARTY IDENTIFICATION BY AGE COHORT

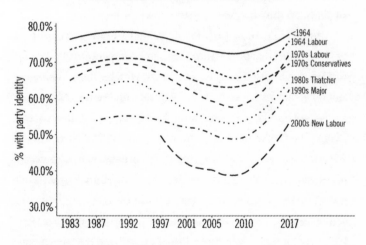

However, the small changes in taste for swinging among the older generations is dwarfed by the promiscuity of the younger generations – shown by the dashed lines – a large proportion of whom never form an attachment to a party at all. Each generation in the data has been less committed to the parties than the previous generation was at the same age, with only around 50 per cent of the youngest generation – those coming of age under New Labour – expressing attachment to any political party.

Since most of this change has been a generational shift, it may be a long road back for the parties. Loyalty to parties is often handed down in families, with children inheriting their parents' commitment to a party. Now that this process has broken down, and younger generations have lost their attachment to parties, they may in turn pass on this political detachment to their children.

The majority of younger voters have simply never grown up with the idea of getting into a long-term relationship with a political party, so they may never settle down.

If Britain's newfound taste for swinging isn't going to disappear any time soon, what does it mean for party competition? In the past most people had settled partisan views, which seldom changed. General elections could be won by attracting the relatively small group of voters who hadn't made up their minds and could very easily vote for either of the two main parties, so political parties based their strategies around mobilising their core voters and targeting the few waverers. While they worried about traditional loyalists not turning up to the polls, the parties could be assured of their supporters' votes as long as they got them to the voting booth.

The electorate is not entirely losing its taste for long-term relationships in politics, though. While voters' attachments to parties are weak, their attachments to sides of the EU referendum are stronger than partisan identity ever was. But these new identities make for much more uncertain election outcomes. While party attachments tended to keep voters faithful, referendum attachments can just as easily pull voters away if another party makes a better offer.

Nowadays, swing voters are no longer a small section of the electorate who are being pulled back and forth by the parties, but a substantial chunk of all voters. This helps to explain why politicians have been so surprised by the sudden rise of new parties competing for groups previously thought to be reliable supporters. The new parties that have entered British politics have also allowed voters to express their views on issues that don't fall neatly into traditional left–right politics such as immigration (UKIP) or Scottish independence (the SNP). This in turn has posed a dilemma for the traditional parties, who are pulled in multiple directions trying to stop their voters being tempted away.

This may just be the start. If the number of swing voters stays this high, the parties will have to get used to defending themselves on multiple fronts.

FURTHER READING

For details of voter switching between 2015 and 2017 see 'Brexit or Corbyn? Campaign and Inter-Election Vote Switching in the 2017 UK General Election' by Jonathan Mellon et al. (*Parliamentary Affairs*, 2018). For a more detailed analysis see *Electoral Shocks: The Volatile Voter in a Turbulent World* by Ed Fieldhouse et al. (Oxford University Press, 2019). Earlier work has also suggested several explanations for these British trends including *Decade of Dealignment* by Bo Särlvik and Ivor Crewe (Cambridge University Press, 1983), and 'The Dynamics of Party Identification Reconsidered' by Harold Clarke and Allan McCutcheon (*Public Opinion Quarterly*, 2009).

'I do see your point of view. But dimly. You see, my own takes up such a lot of the foreground.'

– P. G. WODEHOUSE, *DAMSEL IN DISTRESS*, 1919

—CHAPTER 25—

The average voter is a woman: sex and gender differences

Rosie Campbell

A staple of every election is a discussion of the 'women's vote', as if women are distinct from the 'normal' votes cast. Given that women make up 51 per cent of the whole population and an even greater proportion of eligible voters – and are just as likely to vote as men – the average voter is in fact a woman.

The average voter behaves differently from male voters in some ways. Women are disproportionately represented among undecided voters and they tend to make up their minds who to vote for closer to election day. In 2017, for example, data collected in April and May in the run-up to the election showed that 18 per cent of women said they did not know who to vote for, compared to 10 per cent of men. Women say that they are less interested in politics than men (70 per cent of men and 62 per cent of women reported being interested in politics in 2017), although this gap is reversed when women are asked how interested they are in specific policy areas such as education or health. Women are also more likely to select the 'Don't know' option in political attitude questions and on average score slightly lower than men on political knowledge measures. But, in the end, women are just as likely to vote as men. Indeed, in raw terms, women are slightly more likely to vote than men, although this is due to women's greater longevity combined with higher levels of electoral participation among the old. Turnout among women and men of the same age is pretty similar, but women tend to live longer, so they outnumber men in the growing 'grey' electorate.

There are also consistent sex differences in some political attitudes. Women tend to favour increased taxation and spending on public services more often than men and they are less likely to support cuts in expenditure on key public services (health and education in particular), perhaps unsurprisingly as such spending cuts have a larger impact on women than on men. Women have more egalitarian views than men on a number of issues: they tend to be more progressive on gender equality and less often express racial prejudice or homophobia than men. And there are differences in what political scientists call salience, the priority men and women attach to particular topics. Women report more concern about education and health, while historically men gave relations with the EU and taxation greater priority, though in recent years the gap in strength of feelings about the EU has declined and there was not a significant difference in the way men and women voted in the 2016 EU referendum, although men remain slightly more likely to be more fervently anti-EU than women.

THE BRITISH GENDER GAP 1945–2017

Note: The gender gap above is calculated as the difference in the Con–Lab lead for women and men.

All of the above is well documented. But the truth about women voters is more inconvenient for those of us who would find it easier to trot out a simple story about what women want. The reality is that there is no single story to tell about women voters. They are not some homogenous group that party strategists can target with ease; they are as divided in their opinions as are men. Moreover, although there are differences between women and men in their political behaviour, the similarities are often much stronger. This was especially true when it came to voting – from 1974 onwards, female voters usually behaved in largely the same way as male voters – or at least it was until 2017.

Historically, women voters tended to be slightly more Conservative than male voters. New Labour managed to reduce this disadvantage by picking up the votes of younger women, particularly middle- and higher-income mothers, and in most recent elections the overall picture was one of little or no difference in support for the main parties between the sexes. The figure illustrates the gender gap in support for the two main parties from 1945 to 2017; it is calculated as the difference between the Con–Lab lead for women and for men. A positive score indicates that men are more likely to vote Conservative, a negative score that women are more likely to do so. The decline in Conservative leanings among women voters is apparent, and from 1974 to 2015 the gap rarely reached statistical significance. Given the numbers involved, these differences may still affect the election outcome, but the differences were small enough that variations in the gender gap from one survey to the next might just be due to random error.

But in 2017 we saw the first election where the British Election Study found significantly fewer women voting Conservative than men, while the Labour Party was 8 percentage points ahead among women compared to men. This produces a 12-point gender gap, larger than that seen in any election since the 1950s, and in the opposite direction to the gender gaps seen in earlier elections.

This reversal of the traditional party gender gap might represent a tipping point where the UK's electoral politics begins to mirror that of the United States, where more average voters than men have supported the Democratic presidential candidate in every election since 1980. However, before announcing that the American gender voting gap has come to the UK we should exercise a little caution, both because 2017 was merely one election and because of the unique circumstances of that one election, in which a late swing played such a large part in the result, since that late swing that will have involved more women than men changing their minds.

So, we cannot tell at this stage whether 2017 was a blip or the start of a more fundamental realignment in British politics, with the gender gap flipping directions. Either way, election strategists would be best advised not to ignore the potential for average voters to drive election results.

FURTHER READING

For an excellent discussion of gender and vote in the 2017 election see 'Women, men, and the 2017 general election' by Jane Green and Chris Prosser, available on the British Election Study website. Other useful sources on gender and voting in Britain are Rosie Shorrocks's 'Modernisation and government socialisation: Considering explanations for gender differences in cohort trends in British voting behaviour' (*Electoral Studies*, 2016) and Rosie Campbell's 'What do we really know about women voters? Gender, elections and public opinion' (*Political Quarterly*, 2012). For an analysis of the relationship between gender and the vote in an international context see Ronald Inglehart and Pippa Norris's 'The developmental theory of the gender gap: women and men's voting behaviour in global perspective' (*International Political Science Review*, 2000).

CHAPTER 26

A demographic time bomb: the right and ethnic diversity

Nicole Martin

Ethnic minority electorates are causing headaches for right-wing party strategists across Europe and North America. Ethnic minorities are on average younger than the rest of the population and, with a few exceptions, tend to vote reliably for left-wing parties. As minority electorates grow, they will pose a growing, perhaps existential, challenge for parties of the right: how to appeal to ethnic minority voters, without alienating white voters who are sceptical of immigration and multiculturalism?

The loyalty of ethnic minority voters to left-wing parties is so strong that some have termed it an 'Iron Law'. But it is not a blind or unthinking loyalty. In Europe, left-wing parties have usually been the first to put forward ethnic minority candidates, and tend to have more minority representatives. Although trade unions were initially hostile to minorities – supporting white workers who did not want to work with black workers – left-wing parties have generally been more welcoming of immigrants, and pioneered anti-discrimination laws that helped ethnic minorities access better housing and jobs.

Perhaps most importantly, as ethnic minorities become a greater share of the electorate, they also make up an increasing share of left-wing parties' supporters. In 2010, ethnic minorities were 21 per cent of Labour voters, but just 5 per cent of Conservative ones. To put the figures another way, there were about four and a half times more ethnic minority Labour voters than Conservative ones in 2010. Reliable data on 2015 or 2017 is harder to come by, but what data we have suggests a similar pattern.

The association between ethnic minority voters and left-wing parties is also present in a wide range of countries with very different political systems. In the 2012 US presidential election, 93 per cent of black and 71 per cent of Latino voters supported Barack Obama, in contrast to just 39 per cent of white voters (as discussed further in Chapter 43). Just before the 2013 German federal elections, 50 per cent of Turkish voters expected to vote for the Social Democrat Party, who went on to win only 29 per cent of the vote of the wider electorate. In the Netherlands, the association is so strong that one Dutch council was forced to redesign its strategy to increase ethnic minority turnout when its opponents pointed out that this would almost only benefit the governing left-wing party.

However, many right-wing politicians take comfort in the notion that ethnic minority voters will switch to the right as racial prejudice declines, and second- or later-generation voters find themselves in middle-class jobs, surrounded by high-achieving white voters who lean right. The British Conservative Party has been trying to reach out to south Asian voters since the 1970s – considering these voters to be a natural constituency due to their conservative social values and high rates of small business ownership. They cite recent increases in support from Indian and Pakistani voters as evidence that such a strategy is starting to pay dividends. The German right-wing Christian Democrats similarly increased their vote among ethnic Turkish voters at the 2013 federal elections. Meanwhile in Canada, the Conservatives convinced many minority voters to break their loyalty to the Liberals by the 2010 elections. As the ethnic minority electorate is increasingly made up of the native-born children of immigrants, rather than their parents, who faced more discrimination on arrival and tend to be employed in working-class occupations, minority voters have become more similar to right-wing white voters: more middle-class, more suburban, wealthier.

However, a cautionary tale from the US should sober those who assume that ethnic minority voters will slowly but surely desert the left as they move into middle-class suburbia. In 1996, 74 per cent of Asian Americans supported the Republican candidate Bob Dole. By 2012, this had reversed, with Obama winning 73 per cent of the Asian-American vote and Clinton winning 79 per cent in 2016. The reason? Current Republican hostility to immigrants sits uneasily with Asian-American voters. Despite on average having higher earnings, Asian Americans face prejudice and discrimination just as other minorities do. The problem for right-wing parties is that often their leadership expresses attitudes and promotes policies that are popular with white voters, for example those worried about immigration, but which do not sit well with minority voters – something very evident in the 2016 US presidential election.

The Canadian Conservatives' success in winning over minority

voters was achieved by highly targeted policies at specific immigrant groups – such as lifting certain visa restrictions or apologising
for a past levy that was only applied to Chinese immigrants – yet
when facing defeat in the 2015 election, the party's representatives once again succumbed to the temptation to play to white
voters' anxieties, putting forward a number of anti-Muslim policies. This did not save them on polling day, and squandered the
minority voter goodwill they had worked hard to build up. Indeed,
it is not just right-wing parties that harm their appeal to ethnic
minority voters in this way. The German Social Democratic Party
(SPD) discovered this to their cost in 2010, when Berlin's former
finance minister published a book called (in translation) 'Germany
Does Itself In' in which he claimed that German Muslims rely too
much on social services, and are of lower intelligence. Although
the book struck a chord with many white voters, it damaged the
SPD's standing among Muslim voters. This is the paradox parties
face: they cannot easily respond to white voters' concerns over
immigration and identity without antagonising rapidly growing
ethnic minority electorates.

So ethnic diversity is a challenge for parties in general, but
right-wing parties in particular, who start at a disadvantage with
minority voters. How can such parties win the trust of ethnic
minority voters while also retaining white voters uneasy with
social change? One option may simply be to wait. Later generations of ethnic minority voters, who have faced less racial prejudice
than their parents, access middle-class jobs and do not associate
the centre-right as strongly with racism and xenophobia, may be
more willing to give such parties a hearing. For the same reasons,
the left cannot take ethnic minority loyalty for granted. Parties

of the left will still retain many minority voters, not least because we tend to learn our politics from our parents – but as the ethnic minority electorate diversifies in experiences and attitudes, right-wing parties will find an opportunity developing.

FURTHER READING

For an overview of ethnic minority political behaviour in Great Britain see *The Political Integration of Ethnic Minorities in Britain* (Oxford University Press, 2013), by Anthony F. Heath et al. Evidence of the continuing support of ethnic minority voters for Labour can be found in 'Ethnic minority voters in the UK 2015 general election' by Nicole Martin (*Electoral Studies*, 2018). For research that shows diversity of political opinion among Germany's immigrant-origin ethnic minorities see Kroh and Tucci's 'The Party Identification of Germany's Immigrant Population: Parties Should Not Fear Eased Naturalisation Requirements' (2010).

—CHAPTER 27—

A growing class divide: MPs and voters

Oliver Heath

The number of women and ethnic minority MPs in Parliament has risen sharply over the last few elections, something which has attracted plenty of media attention. Less notice has been paid to another shift in the social mix of the Commons: the decline in the number of working-class MPs. In 1964, 20 per cent of MPs had a working-class occupational background, but by 2017 less than 2 per cent did. This decline is almost entirely due to changes which have occurred within the Labour Party, a party established to ensure working-class representation. In 1964, Labour was not just a party that saw itself as for the working class, but actually was substantially composed of working-class politicians, with 37 per cent of its MPs coming from manual occupational backgrounds. By 2017 this figure had fallen to just 2 per cent.

The changes in the occupational background of MPs within the Labour Party are in part the result of a conscious electoral strategy. Labour selected more and more middle-class candidates to run for office during the 1980s and 1990s as part of an effort to rebrand the party and appeal to middle-class voters put off by Labour's perceived closeness to trade unions and working-class radicalism. The resulting changes in MPs' occupational background have made Parliament less representative of the broader British population, and the Labour Party much less representative of the working class whose interests it was traditionally supposed to champion.

Does this change matter? A growing body of research indicates that it does. Perhaps most importantly, working-class MPs are more likely to represent the interests of working-class voters than MPs from other backgrounds. For example, welfare reforms adopted by the Labour Party under the leadership of Tony Blair were much more likely to be opposed by working-class Labour MPs than they were by their middle-class counterparts, who were much more supportive of the cuts. This finding suggests that the large shift from working-class MPs to middle-class career politicians in the Labour Party considerably weakened the representation of working-class voters' interests.

Survey evidence collected since 1964 also indicates that the decline of working-class MPs within the Labour ranks has substantially reduced the relative popularity of the party among working-class voters, even after controlling for a host of other factors. Working-class people are much more likely than middle-class people to vote Labour when the party contains a substantial number of working-class MPs, and variation over time in the number of working-class Labour MPs closely tracks the strength of such class voting. Working-class voters also tend to be more likely than the middle class to vote Labour when the local Labour candidate is working class, and working-class voters are more likely to regard Labour as being left-wing when they have a working-class Labour candidate in their constituency.

While experiments varying prospective MPs' backgrounds reveal everyone is put off by very wealthy candidates, it is people from a working-class background who are particularly repelled, especially when it comes to judging how approachable candidates are. MPs from privileged backgrounds are indeed perceived as less 'in touch' by working-class voters, who will regard a pledge to stand up for the underprivileged as more credible coming from someone whose own background is modest than a similar promise coming from the child of millionaires. By extension, a party which contains many working-class MPs will be seen by working-class voters as more likely to effectively stand up for their interests.

Although the loss of working-class MPs has not hurt Labour electorally overall – and may even have paid off in terms of making them more appealing to many middle-class voters, at least during the Blair years – it has come at the cost of participatory equality. As the Labour Party has become more middle-class, working-class people have become less likely to vote at all. According to the British Election Study, in 2017 the difference in reported turnout between the working class and the middle class was 18 percentage points, compared to less than just 5 percentage points in 1964.

Indeed, by 2010 the impact of class on turnout was greater than the impact of class on vote choice, an effect which has persisted since. Class is now more important as a participatory divide than it is as an electoral divide. This represents an important milestone in British political history. Traditionally Britain was regarded as *the* class society, where class was pre-eminent among the factors used to explain party allegiance. In comparative terms, the impact of class on vote in Britain has long been unusually high – and was one way in which Britain stood apart from the USA, where class did not divide the parties, but did divide voters from non-voters. The middle-class-focused centrism which Tony Blair learned from Bill Clinton made Britain more like America in an unexpected way: working-class voters have responded here, as they did in the US, by turning their backs on the electoral process altogether.

However, this growing constituency of alienated working-class voters did not stay demobilised for long. The greater pool of working-class voters who were electorally available created fertile ground for populist mobilisation. Many of these voters gave their support to UKIP in the 2015 elections, and then – on the back of Brexit – switched support to the Conservatives in the 2017 elections, when the party received its highest ever share of the working-class vote. The working class are now much more evenly divided between supporting Labour and the Conservatives. The voters New Labour once took for granted have now come to hold a pivotal position in British politics.

FURTHER READING

For a more detailed discussion of the findings discussed here see Oliver Heath's 'Policy Representation, Social Representation, and Class Voting in Britain' (*British Journal of Political Science*, 2015). The survey experiments are discussed in Rosie Campbell and Philip Cowley's 'Rich Man, Poor Man, Politician Man: Wealth Effects in a Candidate Biography Survey Experiment' (*British Journal of Politics and International Relations*, 2014). For a detailed analysis of how the policy preferences of working-class MPs differ from those of middle-class MPs see

Tom O'Grady's excellent 'Careerists Versus Coal-Miners: Welfare Reforms and the Substantive Representation of Social Groups in the British Labour Party' (*Comparative Political Studies*, 2019). And for comprehensive analysis of the changing political significance of class see Geoffrey Evans and James Tilley's *The New Politics of Class: The Political Exclusion of the British Working Class* (Oxford University Press, 2017).

—CHAPTER 28—

We don't do God? Religion and vote choice in Britain

James Tilley

In 2003 Alastair Campbell famously interrupted an interview with Tony Blair to tell the journalist that 'we don't do God'. That succinctly summarises the role of religion in elite political discourse in Britain over the last fifty years. Very few politicians refer to religion and very few, ironically with the exception of Tony Blair, are overtly religious. This is perhaps not surprising as Britain is a largely secular country and the role of religion in post-war politics has generally been perceived as weak. This perception is wrong.

In fact, religion has long been a good predictor of how people vote, and it remains so today. If we look at survey data stretching back to the early 1980s, there are large and constant differences between different religious denominations in their party preferences. Moreover these are in the opposite direction to the differences that we see on the continent. In France, Poland or Spain, practising Catholics are much more likely to support parties of the right, whereas British Catholics vote for the left. As the figure below shows, in England

SEX, LIES AND POLITICS

and Wales, the gap between Catholics and practising Anglicans in
their support for Labour is a consistent 25 percentage points. In
Scotland, this gap was even larger, with three quarters of Catholics
regularly voting Labour before the party's collapse in 2015, compared
to only a third of practising Presbyterians. Those with no religion,
and non-conformists in England (not shown in the graph), tend to
lie somewhere between these two extremes. As an aside, the recent
change for those with no religion in Scotland is due to the sharp rise
of the SNP among that group. This predated the 2015 surge in SNP
support, which was particularly marked among Catholics.

One obvious explanation for these religious differences might
be that they are simply the disguised effects of class, or other social
characteristics like age. If Catholics are more working-class than
Anglicans, then the explanation for Catholics voting Labour may be
their class not their religion. This is not the case. Holding constant
a large array of different social characteristics like class, income,
education, region and so forth, differences in party choice by religious denomination remain. The other obvious explanation is that
people in different denominations have different values, different
policy attitudes and different national identities, and it is these
which explain their vote choices. Again, this is not the case. Holding
constant people's levels of social conservatism, economic leftism
and national identity still does not reduce religious differences.

An alternative explanation is that these voting patterns are a leg-
acy of the religious divisions of the nineteenth and early twentieth
centuries. Before the universal franchise and the emergence of the
Labour Party, when only a minority of men could vote, and cast their
votes for the Liberals or Conservatives, religious denomination was
important. The Liberals were clearly aligned with non-conformists

in the nineteenth and early twentieth centuries. This was related not just to the disestablishment of Anglicanism in Wales, but also education policy and the temperance movement. Conversely, the Conservatives were seen as the party of the Church of England. The Church of England was the established church, and the Conservatives were the party of established privilege.

LABOUR SUPPORT BY RELIGION OVER TIME

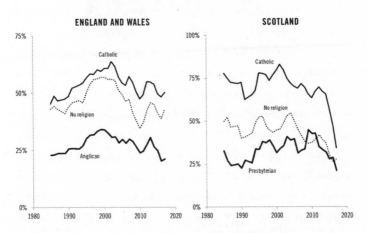

Note: The graphs show three year moving averages of the proportion of people who identify with the Labour party over time as a proportion of party supporters. Presbyterian refers to practising members of the Church of Scotland (those who attend church a few times a year or more) and Anglican refers to practising members of the Church of England (again, those who attend church a few times a year or more). Catholic refers to everyone who identifies themselves as Catholic regardless of religious practice. Data comes from the British Social Attitudes Surveys 1983–2016 and the British Election Survey 2017.

These relationships were then complicated by the emergence of the Labour Party, which explicitly mobilised Catholics as the party grew in the early twentieth century. This was related to the issue of Irish home rule, which Labour supported, but also the fact that Catholics in Britain were predominantly working-class Irish immigrants who would naturally support the new workers' party. Denominations were linked to different parties in a particular way, and this is the pattern that remains today. Catholics in Britain, unlike in other European countries, are still more likely to support the left. Equally, non-conformists are still somewhat more likely to support the Liberals, and practising members of the established churches in both Scotland and England are more likely to support the establishment party of the Conservatives. The denominational patterns that we still see today in England, and saw until very recently in Scotland, are the same patterns evident in the late nineteenth and early twentieth centuries.

Why did these differences persist? One crucial mechanism is inheritance. Religion maintains its link with party loyalties via parental socialisation into both a religious and party identity when children are growing up. People who are successful in passing on their religion to their children also tend to be successful in passing on their partisanship. Religious voting is thus a relic of past associations between groups and parties: religious divisions remain because religion is a marker of parents' and grandparents' party affiliation in an era when religion did matter for policy choices and for voters. Divisions that seem to be built on very little today can ironically be more resilient than those, like class, that seem to be built more firmly on the self-interest of contemporary voters.

Of course, there are some important caveats to all this. First, fewer and fewer people are religious. In that sense, religion at the next election will play a smaller role than it did fifty years ago. Nonetheless, there is still a sizeable minority of people in Britain with a religious identity, and the divisions between denominational groups in England and Wales are still strong. Second, while non-Christian religions make up only a small percentage of the population, they are growing in number and are very distinctive in their voting patterns. Around 5 per cent of the British electorate identify as Muslim, and over 80 per cent of Muslims who voted in 2017 supported Labour. Much like Catholics a century ago, Muslim immigrants have been attracted to the Labour Party for reasons of policy (on immigration and race relations) and economics (Muslim immigrants tend to be poorer). It therefore seems reasonable to think that the trajectory of Muslim voters will be similar to Catholics. Third, parties can sometimes appeal to, or repel, religious voters with their rhetoric or policy. Historically, British Jews have been more likely to support Labour, but the continued association of Labour with antisemitism over the past few years has meant that this group has swung to the Conservatives. In 2017, nearly three quarters of Jewish voters supported the Conservatives. These three points only underline the surprising, but important, role that religion plays in British voting behaviour.

FURTHER READING

For the origins of political divisions based on religion in Britain see Kenneth Wald's book *Crosses on the Ballot* (Princeton University Press, 1983). For more recent accounts of how religion continues to shape politics in Britain see 'We Don't Do God? Religion and Party Choice in Britain' by James Tilley (*British Journal of Political Science*, 2015) and *Religion and Public Opinion in Britain* by Ben Clements (Palgrave Macmillan, 2015). For more detail of how religion affects politics in European countries see the edited volume *Religion and Mass Electoral Behaviour in Europe* (Routledge, 2000) or *Sacred and Secular* by Pippa Norris and Ronald Inglehart (Cambridge University Press, 2004).

CHAPTER 29

Why ethnic minorities vote Labour: group norms

Anthony Heath

Peter Pulzer once famously wrote, 'Class is the basis of British politics; all else is embellishment and detail.' Those days are long gone, and one of the embellishments has overtaken class as the most powerful social cleavage in British politics: ethnic background is now a much more powerful predictor of how people will vote than social class. At the 2010 general election, for example, Labour won only 29 per cent of the popular vote while the Conservatives won 36 per cent – an overall Conservative lead of 7 points. Labour did slightly better among the working class, where 41 per cent voted Labour and 31 per cent voted Conservative – a Labour lead of 10 points. In striking contrast, 68 per cent of ethnic minority voters gave their support to Labour, and only 16 per cent supported the Conservatives – a whopping lead of 52 points. This is the last election for which we have top-quality data on the ethnic minority vote, but what evidence we have from more recent elections indicates that this pattern remains broadly true.

There were hints that the Conservatives made some gains in the 2015 election, especially among the Indian Hindu group, but the party then seemed to slip back in 2017. Ipsos MORI's polling data from 2017 showed the Conservatives winning only 17 per cent of the minority vote against Labour's 73 per cent – a 56-point lead.

The remarkable Labour loyalty of ethnic minorities could have major long-term implications for the party system, as Britain's minority communities are growing rapidly and are set to become a larger and larger proportion of the electorate in the future (as discussed in Chapter 26).

How are we to explain this overwhelming and stable ethnic minority support for Labour? One of the standard accounts of vote choice focuses on matching voters' policy preferences to parties' policy offers. On this account, voters will back the party which has policies most in tune with their preferences on the issues they care about most.

PERCENTAGE FAVOURING THE 'PROGRESSIVE' SIDE OF THE DEBATE

Spending on health and services	49	37
Redistributing wealth	66	45
Allowing strong trade unions	62	56
Protecting rights of the accused	15	22
Detention without trial	33	57
Sending asylum seekers home	39	50
War in Afghanistan	64	56

So we could try to explain minority support for the Labour Party by the extent of fit between the party's and minorities' positions on the issues to which minorities give highest priority. If minorities have distinctive policy preferences, and if Labour policy is closely in tune with these preferences, then this could potentially explain their Labour loyalty. The table opposite shows how minorities and white British voters compared on a number of major issues in 2010.

The table shows some differences, although not in the expected direction: on the classic 'left–right' issues which have historically divided the electorate, such as government spending and the redistribution of wealth, minorities are actually less 'leftist' than the white British. To be sure, minorities were then considerably more progressive on detention without trial and on asylum seekers, although these were not issues on which the Labour governments of this period were especially progressive. If anything, these issues might lead minorities to oppose Labour policy. The only issue on which minorities were more likely than the white British to support Labour policy was the war in Afghanistan, although on this issue there were major differences between minority groups. So, on this evidence, it is not obvious that minorities actually supported Labour at all on the basis of policies, and certainly not by the huge margins described earlier.

Perhaps we are thinking about the issue in the wrong way. Voters might not focus on a party's policies right now but instead consider the whole history of their experiences with different parties. Morris Fiorina once noted, 'Citizens are not fools. Having often observed political equivocation, if not outright lying, should they listen carefully to campaign promises? … In order to ascertain whether the incumbents have performed poorly or well, citizens need only calculate the changes in their own welfare.'

Fiorina's argument was that voters judge what parties have actually done for them in the past, updating their 'tallies' as they go along, giving more weight to recent experiences but still attaching some importance to events long ago. This offers a more promising account of minority support for Labour. All the landmark legislation designed to protect minority interests, such as the 1965, 1968 and 1976 Race Relations Acts and the 2000 Race Relations (Amendment) Act, have been passed under Labour governments.

In contrast, Conservative governments have been notable for their legislation restricting migrant entry rights and making access to citizenship more difficult. While Theresa May set up the Race Disparity Audit when she became Prime Minister, the Conservatives' reputation among minority voters will have been further tarnished by the 2018 Windrush scandal, which involved the wrongful deportation from the UK by the Home Office of long-term resident black British citizens. It served to highlight the hostile environment towards migrants which the Home Office had institutionalised.

These histories of the parties' engagement, or lack of engagement, with minority concerns must be a major part of the story. However, it is not at all clear whether Fiorina's emphasis on the individual citizen's own experiences is right. On an individualistic account, we would expect that a migrant who had only recently arrived in Britain, and who therefore had had little personal experience of Labour's past efforts to improve minority welfare, would be much less likely to support the party than a longer-established voter who had seen and experienced the changes brought about, for example, by the landmark 1976 Act.

In line with the theory, we find that migrants who arrived in Britain a long time ago are slightly more likely to support Labour than the most recent arrivals. But even the most recent arrivals were still overwhelmingly Labour supporters.

So, we have to find an explanation that can account for the Labour loyalties of newly arrived ethnic minority voters. Individualistic explanations clearly fail, and hence the natural alternative is to turn to explanations which take account of the social milieu in which voters find themselves. When a migrant arrives in Britain, he or she will typically be joining an established ethnic community, which will have developed over time many shared norms and sentiments. Migrants do not have to wait to find out for themselves what life would be like under different governments; they will quickly pick up ideas about the British political situation from their new community. Community norms and sentiments, then, may well perpetuate the belief, based on collective experience, that Labour looks after ethnic minorities while the Conservatives do not. And new arrivals will be introduced to these ideas, rather than having to acquire the information for themselves.

Group-based explanations of this kind have become much less popular than they once were, reflecting not only changes in intellectual fashion towards more individualistic choice-based theories but also real changes in British society, which has seen the disappearance of distinctive class-based communities founded on heavy industries, and the rise of more fragmented and mobile careers. But while communities based on social class may have declined or weakened, there are undoubtedly strong communities based on ethnicity in Britain today.

FURTHER READING

A full treatment of this topic, and an account of the data on which it is based, can be found in Chapter 6 of *The Political Integration of Ethnic Minorities in Britain* by Anthony Heath et al. (Oxford University Press, 2013). Important recent work examining ethnic minority voting in the 2015 and 2017 general elections includes Nicole Martin's 'Ethnic minority voters in the UK 2015 general election: a breakthrough for the Conservative party?' (*Electoral Studies*, 2019), Maria Sobolewska's 'Is Labour losing the ethnic minority vote?' and the report by British Future entitled 'Mind the Gap: how the ethnic minority vote cost Theresa May her majority'.

—CHAPTER 30—

When racism stopped being normal, but no one noticed: generational value change

Danny Dorling

How can you tell when the times are changing and great progress is being made, or when we instead appear to be going back in time – 'going back to '79', as the lyrics of a tribute song to the recent Conservative government suggested? Often it feels as if it was mostly in the past that great steps forward were taken. However, it was probably the case that at those times people did not realise that they were achieving much. The same may be true today.

Anxieties and social conflicts fuel a belief that Britain is becoming a less tolerant society. In some of the most unequal rich countries, such as the UK and the US, benefit levels are now so low compared to average wages, that people will do almost any job, or more than one job, to avoid having to claim the dole. The government complains that locals won't do the jobs immigrants will still do. The environment is nasty, and worries about immigration have become highly ranked in what was most important at each forthcoming election.

In this environment you might expect people to become increasingly intolerant of others – people from different groups who could be taking 'their' jobs. The following graph challenges that assumption. It shows the slow but steady decline in opposition to mixed-race marriages, a good indicator of racial prejudice. A generation ago, in 1983, a majority of white British respondents expressed discomfort with the idea of having in-laws from a different race. By 2013, this figure had fallen to less than a quarter.

SHARE OF BRITISH RESPONDENTS EXPRESSING DISCOMFORT ABOUT AN ASIAN OR WEST INDIAN IN-LAW, 1983–2013 (%)

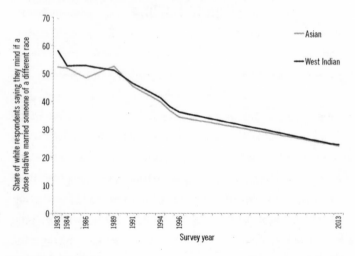

Source: British Social Attitudes.

What the graph shows is that some things change slowly and steadily in a way that is almost impervious to immediate events. This is because much of this slow shift is produced by generational change. Older voters, whose views were shaped by growing up in an almost all-white Britain prior to larger-scale immigration, are very strongly opposed to inter-racial marriage – in 2013 over 40 per cent of those born before 1940 disapproved of it. Opposition is much lower among their children, born in the '60s, and vanishes almost entirely among their grandchildren: less than one in ten of those born in the '90s express any discomfort about having an in-law from a different race.

The graph shows that attitudes can become radically more tolerant, even in times of rising inequality and social conflict. Hostility to minorities fell during the early '90s, despite a recession and mass unemployment, and fell in the 2000s despite the rise in BNP/UKIP voting and widespread public anxiety about immigration. It is possible that the brief hiatus in the rise in tolerance in the mid-'80s was related to the experience of mass unemployment and rapidly growing economic inequalities then, or a birth cohort effect, but what is most important about it is its brevity.

Your parents could well be among those who objected to mixed-race marriages. But if they were growing up in the Britain of the '40s then they were normal. Among younger people today, few worry about whether folk get married or not, or to whom – male or female, black or white. But not long ago it was as normal to be a bigot as not.

Exactly the same has been seen in the US. In the late '50s in the US, twenty-four people disapproved of mixed-race marriage for every one who approved. By the late '60s, that ratio had plummeted to 4:1. By 2012 the *approval* ratio had reached 6:1.

In 1990, 65 per cent of whites in the USA opposed a black–white marriage and 40 per cent opposed an Asian–white or Hispanic–white marriage. By 2008, that had dropped to 25 per cent of US whites opposing a black–white union in their immediate family, and by 2013 just 16 per cent. Then, between 2013 and 2017, the proportion of Americans who said they worried a great deal about race relations rose very rapidly from 17 per cent to 42 per cent, as Trump campaigned for and won the presidency. But as yet we have no evidence of any fall in approval rates for mixed marriage.

Times may seem bad again now, but have a little sympathy for your parents. Just look at what was common in the time of *their* parents, who grew up in a generation of British imperial rule, fascists ruling half of Europe and blackshirts marching in the streets in London. And now have a think about how the generations to come might view your generation. Look at how quickly attitudes are still changing. In a generation's time your views on whether we should worry about how few young men go to university or the sanctity of national borders or the theory that the very wealthy create jobs by investing their wealth could all easily be perceived as sad statements of the ignorance of our times. Whatever it turns out to be, it will be a view that is widespread today but will come to be seen as misguided in the near future.

Looking at past trends in changing attitudes helps us to see how much views that appear to be very fixed can change over the course of lifetimes and between generations. Politics often appears to be in a desperate mess. Progress is slow. Many things are getting worse. But we tend to concentrate on the bad news and on the most powerful, immediate crises. That is how we improve our political lives. We complain and agitate about what matters to us right now, even as other things continue to change and often improve. We might well look back in the future at the years just before and after the 2008 economic crash and say: 'That was when the tide of social change began to accelerate.'

If the analysis of the figures above is right, especially in terms of recent US trends on public opinion, the tide may also be changing, not just in relation to the tolerance of mixed-race marriages and what that implies for the diminishing of racism, but perhaps also in many other areas that currently do *not* look encouraging in contemporary data.

FURTHER READING

This chapter is based on two articles that the author worked on in 2013: 'Tolerance, inequality and the recession' (Sheffield Political Economy Research Institute Blog, 2013) and 'It is necessarily so' (*Significance*, 2013), both of which use data from the USA. For a proper introduction you should read 'The Better Angels of Our Nature: How the Antiprejudice Norm Affects Policy and Party Preferences in Great Britain and Germany' by Scott Blinder et al. (*American Journal of Political Science*, 2013). The American data has been updated using work by Frank Newport ('In U.S., 87% Approve of Black-White Marriage, vs. 4% in 1958'), Art Swift ('Americans' Worries About Race Relations at Record High') and Lawrence Bobo et al. ('The Real Record on Racial Attitudes').

—CHAPTER 31—

Voting together: why the household matters

David Cutts

O f all the contexts where people's identities, norms and attachments are shaped, it is the household that reigns supreme. It is
the prime location for political discussion and decision-making,
and the primary context where individuals obtain and reinforce
their political values, norms and preferences.

People who live together are more likely to take their political
cues from one another, and it is through such discussion that the
social norms of voting, or not voting, are established within families. Simply put, living together leads to shared behaviour. When
one person in a household votes then, as a rule, so too do all the
others: 'Those who live together vote together.' More than nine
out of ten people who lived in a multi-person household where
someone voted also voted themselves in the 2010 general election. Less than one in ten did so when living with a non-voter. Of
course, shared propensities to vote in families may arise because
those who live in the same household are more alike, sharing

socio-economic characteristics, values, attitudes and exposure to campaigning by parties. But even where household members hold dissimilar attitudes, interpersonal interaction in the household over time has been shown to weaken differences, with family members becoming more alike. A strong relationship still exists between the turnout and party choices of one household member and that of the others. Not only does shared partisanship with other household members increase turnout, but the civic duty of other household intimates also drives voting (as discussed in Chapter 23), even when accounting for an individual's civic duty and their similar social backgrounds or political attitudes.

Some household relationships are more important than others, and exposure to these varies through the course of life. There is strong evidence of a link between the political inclinations of husbands and wives, with spouses three times as influential as other relationships. The frequency of political discussion with a spouse also has a positive effect on voter turnout. Married people participate in greater proportions than those who are single, divorced, separated or living with a partner, as they have been found to place greater emphasis on traditional values such as civic duty. The effect of divorce, for instance, can depress turnout by as much as 10 percentage points. Married couples also have high levels of agreement, which increase over time. 'Get out the vote' studies also find that the majority of any effect from voter mobilisation campaigns passes on to other members of the household. Unsurprisingly, the influence of parents over children is also well established, although mothers have a stronger effect on the political preferences of their offspring than fathers. In studies where both the mother and the father support the same party, their child is three times as likely to support it too. Where parents' party choices differ, the child is up to ten times more likely to choose the same party as the mother than that of the father. This positive reciprocal relationship stems from the greater frequency of interaction, regularity of political discussion and the numerous learning opportunities with the mother.

The household is especially important for the socialisation of young people. The young are more easily influenced by others because they have not yet formed habits of voting or not voting, paying attention to politics or tuning it out. The majority of first-time voters live with their parents – the most important socialisation agents – and, as such, the decision of young first-time electors to vote is highly dependent on the participation choices of others in their family. This effect can be either positive or negative: disengaged parents produce disengaged offspring, while politically active parents pass on their enthusiasm just as effectively. A young first-time elector living in a house where another adult goes out to vote is over five times more likely to vote than a counterpart in a household where nobody else votes (the difference is much smaller for older electors). And these differences still exist even when socio-economic and even attitudinal influences are taken into account. It matters less whether there is one other voter or more than one; it is only necessary for most young people to have one other person around to help persuade them to vote.

The relative effect of living with another voter is much more important for first-time electors than for those in their twenties who have had previous opportunities to vote. This is a consequence of younger people moving away from their parents and living with others with whom they share weaker ties. But as voters

SEX, LIES AND POLITICS

enter their thirties and start families of their own, household influences on voting patterns start to increase again. The process once again goes into reverse as people enter the later stages of their life. Recent research suggests that voter turnout between the ages of sixty and ninety declines by more than 30 percentage points. And while worsening health is part of the explanation, the importance of the household once again comes to the fore. Older citizens tend to live alone more than the general population and so receive less social interaction and encouragement to vote from others. The decline in voting is faster for women, who are generally younger than their spouse and thus have a higher propensity to be widowed and live alone at an earlier age than men. Other research shows that the turnout rate of widowed individuals is 9 percentage points lower than would have been the case if their spouse was still alive, with the drop in participation continuing indefinitely. Close intimates play a vital role in the participation process. Whether you are young or old, democracy begins at the kitchen table. Turning out to vote in elections is highly dependent on whether people live with other voters or not. Put simply, the household matters.

FURTHER READING

For a discussion of which context matters in voting, read David Cutts and Edward Fieldhouse's 'What Small Spatial Scales Are Relevant as Electoral Contexts for Individual Voters? The Importance of the Household on Turnout at the 2001 General Election' (*American Journal of Political Science*, 2009). For the importance of the household on young people see 'The Companion Effect: Household and Local Context and the Turnout of Young People' by the same authors (*Journal of Politics*, 2012). For the influence of the household on voting, duty and partisanship, read *Partisan Families: The Social Logic of Bounded Partisanship in Germany and Britain* by Alan Zuckerman et al. (Cambridge University Press, 2007) and 'Shared Partisanship, Household Norms and Turnout: Testing a Relational Theory of Electoral Participation' by Edward Fieldhouse and David Cutts (*British Journal of Political Science*, 2018).

—CHAPTER 32—

North and south: political geography

Charles Pattie

The fundamental geographic division in modern British elections is well known: the south is blue; the north is red. Southern England outside London elected 31 per cent of all British MPs in 2017 but 53 per cent of Conservatives. By contrast, Scotland, Wales and the north of England provided 41 per cent of all MPs but just 19 per cent of Conservatives. Of the fifty-seven 'big-city' MPs elected in Glasgow, Edinburgh, Cardiff, Birmingham, Liverpool, Sheffield, Manchester, Newcastle, Leeds and Bradford, only six were Conservatives.

At the same time, a majority (55 per cent) of Labour's MPs sit for Wales and the north of England. Just twenty-two represented constituencies in East Anglia and the south outside London. Even the Liberal Democrats, often thought of as less regionally concentrated, draw nearly half of their MPs from London and the south of England, and a third from Scotland. Only two areas broke this north–south divide: London, where forty-nine of seventy-three seats went Labour, and Scotland, a country which was a Labour stronghold till 2010 but has been dominated since 2015 by the SNP.

It hasn't always been like this. In 1951, almost half of Scotland's votes and seats went to the Conservatives, as did a third of seats in the major northern cities, while in the south and east outside London Labour won 42 per cent of the vote (if only 17 per cent of the seats). The figure below shows the difference between the Conservatives' and Labour's percentage shares of the vote in each region in 1951 and 2017. Where the Conservatives lead over Labour, the difference is positive; where they trail, it is negative. It tells a story of a nation dividing: in every English region, the political divide yawns wider in 2017 than it did in 1951, while in Scotland both parties have been equally marginalised by the SNP, a fringe party in 1951.

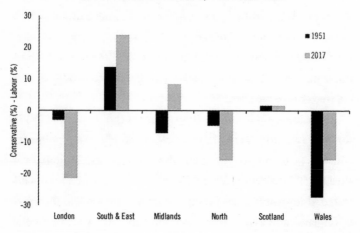

DIFFERENCE BETWEEN CONSERVATIVE AND LABOUR VOTE PERCENTAGES BY REGION, 1951 AND 2017

This geographical polarisation partly reflects social forces. In the '50s, tensions between Roman Catholics (many of Irish descent) and Protestants still influenced politics in the west of Scotland and north-west England. The Conservatives campaigned there as Unionists, giving them an important Protestant working-class support base. Similarly, class voting in mid-twentieth-century Britain influenced the electoral geography, as Labour dominated the working-class communities of the urban and northern industrial centres, while the Conservatives appealed to more middle-class suburban, rural and southern communities.

But outside Northern Ireland religious tensions have since lost their purchase, diminishing Scottish working-class Conservative support. And class is no longer such a major influence on vote anywhere. A stronger explanation for recent shifts in Britain's electoral geography is its changing economic geography. Economic restructuring in the '70s and '80s hit the industrial areas of the Midlands and north hard, while financial services boomed in southern England.

The consequence was that support for the incumbent Conservative government in the 1980s grew in the latter but declined in the former, while Labour support shifted in the opposite direction, widening the gap. When a housing slump in the early '90s hit household wealth in the south, however, the Conservative government's support there waned, narrowing the gap again – by 1997, their vote was 41 per cent in the south-east and 26 per cent in the north: Labour's vote grew in both regions, to 32 per cent and 55 per cent respectively (and remained similar in 2001, when a Labour government was re-elected during a period of economic growth). But not for long: the 2008 economic crisis widened the north–south regional economic divide again, and regional political divides reopened. Seven years later, both parties saw support

grow in most regions (Brexit helped the Conservatives, and Cor-
byn-mania aided Labour), but the regional differences in their
support barely budged. The north–south divide loomed as large
in Corbyn's first election as Labour leader as it did when he first
became an MP thirty-four years earlier.

This has consequences for party strategy. In the '80s, Labour was
increasingly restricted to its northern urban strongholds and had
no prospect of majority government. To regain power, it had to
convince voters further south that it could deliver economic pros-
perity. Achieving this was key to New Labour's three Westminster
majorities in 1997–2005. Only when economic crisis post-2007
undermined Labour's reputation for competence did the party
retreat from the south and the Midlands and, as a result, from
government. A move to the left in 2017 saw the party gain support
in some more middle-class areas, including in London and the
south – but it was not so successful in many of its previous working-class strongholds where Brexit was popular, nor in enough of
the suburban areas where New Labour had appealed, suggesting
it remains very hard for Labour to enter government without a
'middle England' strategy. The Conservatives, too, face a strategic
geographical problem. Now a marginal force in the English urban
north and Wales, they could still (as in 2015) form majority governments based on support in the south and Midlands (though this
would not be easy), but, the 2017 Scottish revival notwithstand-
ing, the party's credentials as a UK-wide force are compromised.

But perhaps the most important consequence of regional
political polarisation has been the steep decline in the number
of marginal constituencies. In the early '50s, 25–30 per cent of all
constituencies were Conservative/Labour marginals, where less

than 10 percentage points separated the two parties. By 2017, this had halved to just 15 per cent of seats. Fewer marginals mean a less responsive electoral system (with larger swings in national vote shares required to unseat incumbent governments) as well as increasing concentration of campaign effort on a few voters in a few key places. As the country becomes politically more divided, the incentives of party competition encourage politicians to talk to ever smaller and more localised groups of voters. As the United Kingdom divides, so fewer places matter.

FURTHER READING

Britain's electoral geography is discussed in Ron Johnston and Charles Pattie's *Putting Voters in their Place: Geography and Elections in Great Britain* (Oxford University Press, 2006) and in 'A re-dividing nation?' by Ron Johnston et al. (*British Politics*, 2017). For an account of the geography of the 2017 election see 'Coming full circle: the 2017 UK General Election and the changing electoral map' by Ron Johnston et al. (*The Geographical Journal*, 2018).

'All politics is local.'

– USUALLY ATTRIBUTED TO TIP O'NEILL, SPEAKER OF THE UNITED STATES HOUSE OF REPRESENTATIVES (1977–87), BUT FIRST USED AS EARLY AS JULY 1932

—CHAPTER 33—

The myth of meritocratic Scotland: political cultures in the UK

Ailsa Henderson

Successive election manifestos from political parties in Scotland have argued that Scots have different values to those in the rest of the UK. More meritocratic, more communitarian, more supportive of state intervention in the economy and EU membership, Scots are portrayed as a left-leaning social democratic foil to an essentially conservative, Eurosceptic, class-bound England. Such comparisons were rife during the Thatcher years but have continued today and feature regularly in the claims made by Scottish politicians and parties. Devolution, argued the Labour Party, would allow Scots to turn their distinct preferences into practice. Independence, argued the SNP repeatedly during the independence referendum campaign, would allow them to do so without the risk of intervention from London.

If we actually look at what people in Scotland, Wales and England think about various policy options or fundamental values we can often identify clear distinctions among them. They back different parties in elections, they hold different national identities. They vary in how well they perceive the current political system to be working (does Scotland/Wales/England get its 'fair share'?) and in the constitutional solutions that they propose. Scottish voters are more supportive of the EU, on some measures at least. Data collected in 2014 for the Future of England Survey show Scots are more likely to believe membership in the EU is a 'good thing', and the 2018 data show an increasing gap between Scotland and England on European attitudes.

However, while Scots voted by a substantial margin to remain in the European Union in 2016, various surveys show that concerns about the European Union and immigration are often not that different between Scotland and England. Data collected in 2014 for the Future of England Survey show Scots don't always have lower levels of Euroscepticism. Data collected in 2017 for the British Social Attitudes Survey show the same levels and distribution of support for immigration. Scots might differ from the English in the conclusions they reach, but on core beliefs there is remarkable similarity.

Much of the rhetoric about distinct political cultures concerns fundamental economic and social values: whether a state should be interventionist or not; whether women with young children should work outside the home; whether the state should support censorship in certain circumstances or ensure resources are redistributed from the rich to poor. On these sorts of issues, and on fundamental evaluations of the state (our sense of trust and sense of efficacy), the claims of distinctiveness typically outstrip results. Scots are not more meritocratic or communitarian than English or Welsh residents. Even where there are differences, they fade once you control for demographic characteristics such as social class. Scots feel differently about the UK, about how well it is run and how it should organise itself, but they don't necessarily feel differently about how a state in general should operate and what it should do for people.

The graph below provides average scores (taken from multiple questions) for three typical measures: a welfarism scale (with higher scores implying support for a more interventionist state); a libertarian–authoritarian scale (higher scores implying greater support for censorship); and a left–right scale (higher scores implying more right-wing). In no case are there significant differences between Scotland, Wales and England.

COMMON VALUES ACROSS SCOTLAND, WALES AND ENGLAND

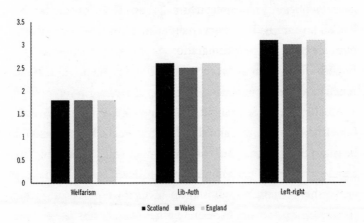

Source: British Social Attitudes Survey, 2017.

So where do these claims of distinct political cultures come from? Some researchers have long argued that this is a north

Britain–south Britain divide, that values still have more to do with social demographic factors such as one's social class, gender or age, and that the distribution of people in different economic circumstances is driving regionalised pockets of support for different values or different policies. There is much merit to this argument.

At the same time, the presence of a Scottish Parliament and a Welsh Assembly means that Scottish and Welsh political parties have a venue in which to articulate perceived differences in values and to legislate on their behalf. And so the perception of value differences between countries, even if it is misleading, can lead to real differences in policy. Legislators who believe in a more communitarian or left-wing Scotland have used such arguments to justify introducing free university education and free personal care for the elderly in Scotland. Perhaps, therefore, the more politically important feature of these distinct values across the regions of the UK is not whether they are true, but whether they are believed to be true.

This distinction between evidence and perception helps to explain the sometimes contradictory results we see in surveys and the arguments among politicians about whether Scottish, Welsh, English or indeed British values exist. When asked to describe whether they are more left- or right-wing, Scots, for example, are significantly more likely to report themselves as being left-wing than other Britons. But when we ask about the types of values that would indicate whether someone is left-wing or not, there aren't usually meaningful differences across the regions of Britain. The 2018 Future of England Survey asked individuals about attitudes to immigration, the redistribution of wealth and prison sentences as well as whether people thought attitudes in their 'region' were more supportive of each of these policies than elsewhere in the UK. The Scottish answers are revealing: although Scottish attitudes are fairly similar to those in England and Wales, Scots believe that they are more supportive of immigration and redistribution and less supportive of stiffer sentences than they actually are. So Scots believe they are distinctively left-wing, their belief in this distinctiveness is reinforced by the rhetoric from politicians and civic organisations, and it then comes to form part of the mental imagery of Scottish national identity. This might explain why, in the 2016 devolved election, Scottish Election Study data show that voters consistently misperceived the tax policies of parties by overestimating how left-wing they were. If being a Scot is less about where you were born and more about the values you hold, does it matter if such distinctive 'Scottish' values don't really exist? And for whom are legislators creating policy: the electors they have, or the electors they think they have? If politicians create legislation based on what they believe their voters value, rather than what they actually value, do they end up creating the electorate they imagine? 'Scottish values' may be more imagined than real right now, but several decades of legislation seeking to reflect such values could further distinguish a Scottish political culture.

FURTHER READING

The political culture classic remains Gabriel Almond and Sidney Verba's *The Civic Culture* (Princeton University Press, 1963). The British and Scottish Social Attitudes surveys have generated useful chapters on regional variations in attitudes, for example John Curtice's 'One Nation Again' in *British Social Attitudes 13* (Dartmouth, 1996). For an account of Scottish political culture see Ailsa Henderson's

Hierarchies of Belonging: National Identity and Political Culture in Scotland and Quebec (McGill-Queen's University Press, 2007). The most recent accounts of English political culture may be found in the Future of England reports, such as Taking England Seriously (CCC, 2014) and analyses of Englishness in the Brexit vote (including 'How Brexit was made in England' by Henderson et al. in the *British Journal of Politics and International Relations*, 2017). For Scotland and Wales see *More Scottish than British* by Chris Carman et al. (Palgrave, 2014) and *Wales Says Yes* by Richard Wyn Jones and Roger Scully (University of Wales Press, 2012).

—CHAPTER 34—

1859 and all that: the enduring failure of Welsh Conservatism

Roger Awan-Scully

1 859: the year of the Austro-Sardinian war; the establishment of Queensland in Australia; and the first chiming of Big Ben. Lincoln's election as US President was still a year away; Queen Victoria's reign was only one-third completed.

1859 was also the last year, to date, when the Conservatives' general election vote share in Wales exceeded that in England. At *every* subsequent election, the Tories have done worse in Wales.

The direct consequence of enduring Conservative failure has been a persistently lopsided electoral politics in Wales. During the later nineteenth century and early years of the twentieth, the obverse of Tory weakness was Liberal strength. Even in difficult years, like the sweeping Conservative victories of 1886, 1895 and 1900, the Liberals remained supreme in Wales. In retrospect, harbingers of change can be seen in the two 1910 elections. Five Welsh Labour MPs were elected in both, and in the latter, the Liberals' vote share fell below 50 per cent, a level it would never again attain.

The divisions that rended the Liberal Party after 1916 helped the substantial 1918 franchise expansion feed not Liberal strength, as pre-war observers might have expected, but Labour instead. With hindsight, Labour's rise can appear inevitable. That wasn't so at the time, and Wales (indeed Britain as a whole) experienced genuine three-party politics between the wars. But this period now appears an interregnum, not only between two cataclysmic conflicts, but between two eras of one-party dominance in Wales.

The 1945 election saw Labour emerge as Wales's dominant political force: winning a majority of Welsh votes and over two-thirds of MPs. Labour's 1945 landslide would not be replicated across the UK until 1997. But its dominance in Wales proved persistent. At every subsequent general election, Labour has won the most Welsh votes and a majority of Welsh seats.

But whoever has been strong in Wales, for over 150 years the Conservatives have always been weak. From 1945 to 2017, their general election vote share was an average of 15.7 percentage points lower in Wales than in England.

And while the Conservatives now underperform in other parts of the UK (such as Scotland and the north of England), within living memory Tory support barely differed between southern and northern England while a (bare) majority of Scots voted Conservative in 1955. Distinct to Wales is the historical consistency of anti-Conservatism. For almost as long as they have been able to vote at all, Welsh voters have shunned the Tories.

Conservative weakness has persisted through vast economic change. Wales was relatively prosperous in the decades preceding 1914, suffered in the appalling, inter-war 'locust' years, and has struggled with relative poverty ever since. Antipathy to the

Conservatives has also long outlasted the main social movements that, some have argued, created and initially sustained it, such as non-conformist Protestantism, which opposed the Conservatives as the party of the Anglican church, and the industrial trade unions, which opposed the Conservatives as the party of capital.

While Wales may be poorer and more working-class than the rest of England, these social differences cannot remotely account for its exceptional voting pattern. Members of all major social groups in Wales (as, indeed, now in Scotland and northern England) are less likely to vote Conservative than their Midlands and southern English counterparts.

Nor is Welsh exceptionalism a product of attitudes. Numerous studies indicate that people in Wales (and, again, in Scotland and northern England, as discussed in the previous chapter) are *not* more radical in their views than the bluer parts of England. Attitudes differ only about the parties themselves, with many voters in all of these regions appearing to view Conservatives as fundamentally alien.

Throughout the era of mass participation elections, Conservatives in Wales have been identified as a largely English party, somehow non-Welsh or even anti-Welsh in orientation, their limited electoral successes in Wales being confined almost entirely to the most heavily 'anglicised' areas. The Tories' opponents – first the Liberals, then Labour – more effectively identified themselves with ordinary Welsh people, including the many who were not 'nationalist' in terms of desiring greater Welsh political autonomy.

Some, in recent decades, have fought to develop a more authentically Welsh Conservatism – notably Wyn Roberts, Welsh Office Minister under Thatcher and Major, who produced the 1993 Welsh

Language Act. But Roberts's efforts were undermined in the late '80s and '90s by the appointment of several Secretaries of State with little connection to (and, in one instance, very obviously no sympathy for) Wales. Nor were Welsh perceptions of the Tories obviously improved by their campaign for the first Welsh Assembly elections in 1999, which evinced continuing hostility to devolution and also the Welsh language. Things only began to improve somewhat after several Welsh Tories (notably Nick Bourne, National Assembly leader from 1999 to 2011) embraced devolution and sought to advance a more positive Welsh Conservative agenda. In the 2010 general election, the gap between Tory vote share in England and that in Wales fell below 14 percentage points for the first time in the post-war era (at 13.5 per cent) and the 2011 National Assembly election produced the Conservatives' best-ever result, overtaking Plaid Cymru to become the main opposition party. By 2017, the general election Conservative vote share gap between England and Wales was down to a 'mere' 12 percentage points.

Yet long-standing perceptions can be difficult to shift. Even by the 2016 Welsh Assembly election, survey evidence from the Welsh Election Study showed that while Labour scored strongly in terms of perceived concern for all major social groups in Wales, the Conservatives were viewed as particularly concerned with the interests of the English. Moreover, the modest recent improvements in Welsh Conservative fortunes have not overturned many decades of one-party domination. Welsh politics remains seriously lop-sided.

Even prior to devolution, one-party dominance mattered for political life in Wales. Control of the Welsh Office periodically changed hands, but sustained Labour electoral supremacy produced organisational stagnation – highly uncompetitive elections in most areas did nothing to uphold vibrant party organisations. And one-party dominance now matters more directly for the government of Wales. By 2021, the Assembly will have completed five full terms, with no period of non-Labour government. The entire menu of options thus far has been Labour governing by itself, or Labour as senior coalition partner. The enduring weakness of Welsh Conservatism has substantially attenuated the centre-right's contribution to politics and policy-making in Wales. And, alongside Plaid Cymru's failure to sustain a serious challenge to Labour since 1999, it means that an end to Labour hegemony in Wales remains elusive.

FURTHER READING

The topic of this essay, like Welsh politics in general, is sparsely analysed. 'Why do the Conservatives always do (even) worse in Wales?' by Richard Wyn Jones et al. (*British Elections and Parties Review*, 2002) explored the Welsh Conservatives' long-standing electoral travails in more detail. Ian MacAllister's 'The dynamics of one-partyism' (*Llafur*, 1980) was written over thirty years ago, but remains relevant to understanding the implications of one-party domination for party politics in Wales. Peter Kellner's 'Why Northerners Don't Vote Tory' considers the Tories' more recent (but similar) difficulties in northern England.

CHAPTER 35

'I didn't understand people who are Nationalists don't vote for Unionist parties and vice versa': a former Secretary of State's guide to Northern Ireland

Jon Tonge

Northern Ireland does not suffer from a lack of politicians. Its electorate of 1.2 million is represented by ninety Assembly members, eighteen MPs and 462 councillors. There are even two First Ministers.

These politicians remain in place regardless of whether their institutions function or they attend. Amidst political wrangling, the Northern Ireland Assembly and Executive have been suspended for 40 per cent of the period since their establishment in 1999, but everyone has continued to be paid. There have even been two elections, in 2003 and 2017, to an Assembly that was not sitting.

Meanwhile, Sinn Féin's MPs continue to refuse to take their seats at Westminster, declining to swear an oath of allegiance to a UK monarch. There is even disagreement over what Northern Ireland should be called. Sinn Féin eschews recognition of the term as it legitimises the partition of Ireland. They prefer 'the North of Ireland', 'the North', or 'the Six Counties'. They used to talk of 'the Occupied Six Counties', so things have moderated recently. The 1998 Good Friday Agreement did away with most political violence, of course – apart from the near 3,000 shooting and bombing incidents and over 150 deaths since.

Yet despite the big reduction in violence, ethno-national division and a sectarian chasm continue to dominate Northern Ireland's elections. Most electors do not identify as 'Northern Irish', only one-quarter adopting the label, more preferring to be seen as 'British' or 'Irish'. Effectively, there are separate communal elections for each contest, one within the Protestant Unionist British tradition; the other within the Catholic Nationalist Irish community, one of the strongest relationships between religion and party choice anywhere in Europe.

At the 2017 general election, the correlation between the total vote for Nationalist parties and the percentage of Catholics in each constituency was 0.99. For the non-statistically minded reader, 1.00 would represent a perfect match, so we are not far away. On the Protestant side, the equivalent score (related to votes for Unionist parties) was 0.96.

The most recent (2018) Northern Ireland Life and Times survey found that only 1 per cent of Protestants described themselves as 'Nationalist', while the percentage of Catholics describing themselves as Unionist was just 2 per cent. The same year's general election saw only 0.3 per cent of Catholics supporting the most popular party in Northern Ireland, the Democratic Unionist Party

(DUP), and only 0.2 per cent of Protestants voting Sinn Féin. Unionist and Nationalist parties have an almost exclusively single-religion base. Catholic membership of the main Unionist party, the DUP, is a mere 0.6 per cent and within the Ulster Unionist Party (UUP) the percentage is even lower, at 0.3.

According to successive Life and Times and election surveys, the largest single category of elector (over 40 per cent) in Northern Ireland is one who loftily declares him/herself to be neither Unionist nor Nationalist. But nearly 90 per cent of votes are for Unionist or Nationalist parties, even though the non-aligned Alliance Party has seen a recent improvement in fortunes. Avowedly non-Unionist, non-Nationalist electors seem either to be the least likely to vote or the least likely to tell the truth to survey researchers.

An electoral spring remains elusive. Westminster's plurality first-past-the-post elections may reinforce this communal voting model by encouraging voters on both sides of the divide to consolidate behind a single sectarian candidate, but there is at least the potential for lower-preference vote transfers across the sectarian divide under the more proportional Single Transferable Vote method used for all other contests. However, the traffic across the divide – Protestants voting for Nationalist parties or Catholics voting for Unionist parties – remains pitifully low. The table shows the low rate of cross-community lower-preference vote transfers since the Assembly was created in 1998.

All this appeared to be news to one Secretary of State for Northern Ireland, Karen Bradley, who, after her appointment in 2018, told *The House* magazine: 'I didn't understand things like when elections are fought for example in Northern Ireland, people who

are Nationalists don't vote for Unionist parties and vice-versa.'
Bradley lasted only eighteen months in the job.

LOWER-PREFERENCE VOTE TRANSFERS ACROSS THE SECTARIAN DIVIDE IN NORTHERN IRELAND, 1998–2017 ASSEMBLY ELECTIONS, AS PERCENTAGE OF AVAILABLE VOTE TRANSFERS

TRANSFER FROM	TRANSFER TO	PERCENTAGE OF AVAILABLE VOTE TRANSFERS
DUP	Sinn Féin	0.2
UUP	Sinn Féin	0.3
DUP	SDLP	4.7
UUP	SDLP	7.8
Sinn Féin	DUP	0.2
Sinn Féin	UUP	0.2
SDLP	DUP	1.1
SDLP	UUP	12.6

Obviously there are more important aspects of communal division
than reluctance to transfer lower-preference votes across a sectarian chasm: the percentages of Northern Ireland's population in
'mixed' marriages and of children attending religiously integrated
schools are both below 15 per cent. Nearly 90 per cent of public
housing is segregated on Protestant–Catholic lines. More than
100 peace walls, physically separating the ethno-religious communities, remain in place, decades after paramilitary ceasefires.
Armed republican dissidents continue to claim the title deeds to
the IRA and occasionally kill.

And if such divisions were not acute enough, cue Brexit: 59 per
cent of Protestants voted to leave the EU in the 2016 referendum;

only 15 per cent of Catholics did likewise. The DUP has always been anti-EU, and 70 per cent of its supporters voted Leave. While the nature of the DUP's Euroscepticism has changed – from suspicions of a Papal conspiracy to issues of sovereignty – its actuality has not. Sinn Féin, meantime, has become more pro-EU. So, even if there was a devolved power-sharing Executive in place, the idea that it could have offered coherence on the burning issue of the day is for fantasists. On Brexit, like so much else, Northern Ireland is polarised.

FURTHER READING

Northern Ireland's electoral polarity and how religious affiliation shapes allegiance is detailed in Jocelyn Evans and Jon Tonge's 'Social Class and Party Choice in Northern Ireland's Ethnic Blocs' (*West European Politics*, 2009). A gentler, election-specific, guide is provided by the same authors in their chapters on Northern Ireland in the *Britain Votes* series (Oxford University Press, 2010, 2015, 2017). For more on Northern Ireland's power-sharing and parties see Brendan O'Leary's *A Treatise on Northern Ireland, Volume III* (Oxford University Press, 2019) and David Mitchell's *Politics and Peace in Northern Ireland* (Manchester University Press, 2015). Annual surveys of Northern Ireland opinion are available via the Northern Ireland Life and Times surveys.

—CHAPTER 36—

Two tower blocks in Dundee: constituency campaigning

David Denver

Back in 1970, John Bochel and I undertook a small experiment in Dundee during the local elections of that year. This was (we think) the first field experiment in British political science and the aim was to test whether local campaigning made a difference to election results. To do this, we selected two tower blocks of flats, situated in a safe Labour ward, equidistant from their polling station. With the co-operation of the local Labour Party – no other party did any campaigning – we canvassed the people in one block thoroughly and 'knocked up' supporters on polling day. Residents of the other received only a single leaflet from the candidate. A follow-up survey found that our 'experimental' block had a turnout 10 percentage points higher than the 'control' block (64 per cent to 54 per cent). Also, in the former Labour's share of the vote was 81 per cent; in the latter it was 77 per cent. These differences were magnified when we examined voters who had been canvassed more than once and/or 'knocked up' on polling day.

Although the results of our experiment were published, we (and a few others) remained voices in the wilderness in suggesting that constituency campaigning made a difference. What used to be called the 'orthodox' view of campaigning in Britain, established in the '50s by the Nuffield election studies, held sway then and did so for another twenty-five years. In this view, modern election campaigns were so dominated by the national mass media and the national party leaders that what happened on the ground in the constituencies was hardly worthy of consideration and certainly had no impact on election outcomes. The Nuffield studies were replete with references to local campaigning as a 'ritual'.

This highly influential judgement was based on what now appears to be remarkably casual research. From the 1955 election onwards, the authors of successive studies asked regional party officials, in advance of the election, to identify constituencies in which their party's local campaign organisation would be particularly good or particularly bad. After the election it emerged that in almost every case electoral change in these constituencies ('swing') was little different from the average. It was concluded that local candidates and local campaigns were at the mercy of the national swing, determined by national factors, and that the many thousands of people who devoted time and energy to working in elections were worthy but somewhat eccentric individuals, maintaining a quaint but really rather pointless tradition.

Since the '90s, however, things have changed remarkably. More rigorous academic research has produced plenty of evidence that local campaigning is not just a 'ritual' but, for the most part, has an electoral payoff. These more recent studies of campaigning fall into two main types: those which relate some measure of campaign intensity across constituencies to election outcomes and those based on surveys of the electorate.

Surveys of election agents, carried out at every general election since 1992, have been used to derive campaign intensity scores across constituencies. Other measures of the strength of local campaigns have been based on surveys of party members and campaign spending across constituencies. Although the studies using these approaches differ on some details and the measures themselves are imperfect, all have shown that parties' efforts pay off: more intense local campaigns produce better results for the parties concerned.

As far as electorate surveys are concerned, it is instructive to note that the British Election Study (BES) report on the 1992 general election has a chapter called 'The election campaign' and within that a section on 'explaining campaign movements'. Nowhere in the chapter is there any reference to on-the-ground campaigning. By 2001, however, after a new team took over the BES, the surveys included batteries of questions investigating exposure to face-to-face canvassing, telephone contact with parties and get-out-the-vote operations on polling day. The analysis found consistent evidence that these local campaign activities mattered.

It should be said that no one is claiming constituency campaigning alone will reverse a clear national swing or that the impact is huge. In 2010, for example, research based on the survey of agents suggested that an above-average Liberal Democrat campaign could boost the party's vote share by 3.7 percentage points while for Labour the figure was 1.7 points and for the Conservatives just 0.8 points. Nonetheless, these are not increases to be sneered at in tight contests. Labour won six seats from the Conservatives by 1.7 points or less in 2010 and the Liberal Democrats seven by 3.7 points or less. If these had all gone to the Conservatives then David Cameron would have been just seven seats short of an overall majority in the House of Commons. Similarly, in 2015, more intense campaigning resulted in a boost of around 1.6 points in the Conservatives' share of the electorate, with Labour and the Liberal Democrats benefiting by 1.4 and 1.8 points respectively. The effects were even greater in seats in which the relevant party was in with a decent chance of winning.

Partly in response to the results of academic research on campaigning effects, party professionals now put much more effort into the constituency battles on the ground than before. Indeed, the 'ground war' is now central to the overall campaign strategy and the campaign activities of each party. In what are identified as key seats, the local effort is now seen as too important to be left to local enthusiasts, and the activities involved have changed dramatically since John Bochel and I tramped up and down stairs in our multi-storey blocks. Computers are now universally used for routine campaign tasks; canvassing (now 'voter ID') is increasingly undertaken by paid employees at central or regional 'telephone banks' rather than face-to-face on the doorstep; individual voters are targeted with direct mail shots or social media organised from the centre. Outside of a few rural areas, public election meetings are virtually unheard of. Nonetheless, local campaigners are still visible on the ground. Leaflets are delivered and party number-takers with their familiar rosettes are still encountered outside polling stations while others are crossing off the names of those who have voted and chasing up laggards. It is pleasing to report that they are not simply maintaining a quaint tradition but helping their party to maximise its electoral support. If any candidates dared to take the old orthodoxy at face value and decided not to bother with a local campaign then they would soon find out how much constituency campaigning matters.

FURTHER READING

The original Dundee experiment is reported in John Bochel and David Denver's 'Canvassing, Turnout and Party Support: An Experiment' (*British Journal of Political Science*, 1971). The 'breakthrough' book on constituency campaigning is *Modern Constituency Electioneering* by David Denver and Gordon Hands (Frank Cass, 1997). The most recent reports based on surveys of election agents are 'The electoral effectiveness of constituency campaigning in the 2010 British general election: The "triumph" of Labour' by Justin Fisher et al. (*Electoral Studies*, 2011) and 'The impact of electoral context on the electoral effectiveness of district-level campaigning: popularity equilibrium and the case of the 2015 British general election' by Justin Fisher et al. (*Political Studies*, 2018). The latter two, however, are not for the statistically faint-hearted. We await similar studies of the many claims made about constituency campaigning in 2017.

—CHAPTER 37—

We know where you live: the importance of local candidates

Jocelyn Evans

When you vote, do you care where the candidates live? Election candidates go out of their way to stress their local connections – however tenuous they may be in some cases – and residence is certainly one measure of localness.

Evidence from other political systems has long revealed an effect based on how local the candidates are. In the '70s and '80s, this was tested in different settings – from New Zealand local elections, to US gubernatorial elections, even US presidential elections with the so-called 'home-state advantage'. Britain, however, was largely overlooked. As the Irish geographer, Anthony Parker, put it, Britain 'often yield[s] unknown and inaccessible public representatives, who are often voted for merely because they are standing for a particular political party'.

But if that's true, why do election candidates go to such efforts to tell you how local they are? A renewed interest in the localism of British candidates has accompanied the reinvigoration of regional and local politics, and the decline of deferential party support. Recent research has been able to test this in two different ways, and both confirm that voters are indeed influenced by how far candidates live from them.

The first approach is to run survey experiments on the electorate, presenting profiles for fictional parliamentary candidates and asking people to compare them on different attributes, such as approachability, effectiveness and electability, while randomly altering the profile of one candidate by age, gender, occupation, education and the like, to measure the effect this can have. Such experiments have managed to dispel some popular misconceptions about candidate preferences, such as voters preferring male to female candidates. But one of the strongest effects comes from comparing a candidate who lives locally to one who lives a substantial distance away – voters overwhelmingly score the local candidate higher across all attributes. In one study, making one of the fictitious candidates live 120 miles away from a constituency, as opposed to living within the seat, was enough to generate a 15 percentage point swing away from that candidate.

The second approach is to test the effect in the field: mapping where voters and candidates live, measuring the distance between them, and then looking for any differences in the likelihood of voting for a candidate. Identifying where candidates and voters live is relatively simple. For general elections, candidates may provide their address in the Statement of Persons Nominated – the list of candidates released with the Notice of Poll before the election – which then appears on the ballot paper.

For the 2015 general election, a YouGov survey provided a sample of the electorate, including a precise residential location (anonymously, of course), as well as a range of more usual predictors of vote – for example, the voter's partisanship, or which candidate if any is incumbent. To add in a simplified version of the experimental approach, the survey also included a measure of how local the respondents thought each candidate was. In 2010, the distance effects had been large – up to a 15 percentage point difference in vote for a nearby and distant Tory, and around 10 points for their Labour counterpart. In 2015, the effect of distance was more muted, but even taking into account the other aspects of localness that might have influenced voters, it still had a discernible effect.

The table shows the size of this effect for the four main parties. The top two lines show the real outcomes – how far on average a Conservative, Liberal Democrat, Labour and UKIP candidate lived from their constituents, and the average share of the vote they won in the 403 constituencies examined. The 'Same' row estimates what would happen if all the candidates lived the same distance away (26 km, the distance we used in the original analysis) and then the four successive scenarios put the candidates one by one 120 km away. For the Conservatives and Labour, this would result in around a 6.5 percentage point drop on their real average share, and around 2 to 3 points for the Liberal Democrats and UKIP.

Why distance mattered somewhat less in 2015 than 2010 is a puzzle. The average distance of our candidates in 2015 is somewhat lower than in 2010. The sample of candidates may have something to do with this, with a 15–20 per cent drop in 2015 on the four-fifths of the main party candidates in 2010 who provided their address on the ballot paper (a figure which dropped even further in 2017). Greater increases in withheld addresses were to be found among candidates living outside their constituency. So, the relatively smaller sample may be biased by being a more local subset of candidates willing to give their address.

VOTES FOR PARTY CANDIDATES AS DISTANCE BETWEEN CANDIDATE ADDRESS AND VOTER ADDRESS CHANGES (%)

	CONSERVATIVE	LIBERAL DEMOCRAT	LABOUR	UKIP
Distance (km)	20.52	16.28	12.86	13.47
Real	53.86	7.28	28.93	9.96
Same	54.40	7.26	28.51	9.86
Far Tory	**47.14**	8.49	33.26	11.15
Far LD	55.46	**5.28**	29.16	10.12
Far Labour	58.82	7.96	**22.45**	10.79
Far UKIP	55.56	7.52	29.41	**7.55**

We should also not overlook that this recent research finds that voters are more likely to vote for candidates they *perceive* as local, be it because of where they live or for whatever other reason. Distance from candidate to voter was never the whole story of localism, then, but it remains one candidate trait which underlines the continued importance of selecting local candidates.

FURTHER READING

The survey experiments can be found in Rosie Campbell and Philip Cowley's 'What voters want: reactions to candidate characteristics in a survey experiment'

(*Political Studies*, 2014). The original 2010 general election test is reported in Kai Arzheimer and Jocelyn Evans's 'Geolocation and voting: Candidate-voter distance effects on party choice in the 2010 UK general election in England' (*Political Geography*, 2012). The 2015 'unified theory' can be found in all four authors' paper, 'Candidate localness and voter choice in the 2015 General Election in England' (*Political Geography*, 2017).

—CHAPTER 38—

The phantoms of Fife: death and voting

Kingsley Purdam

Ronnie Carroll, who died in April 2015 aged eighty, had two claims to fame. He was the only singer to have represented the UK in the Eurovision Song Contest two years in succession, with 'Ring-a-Ding Girl' in 1962 and 'Say Wonderful Things' the year after, coming fourth on both occasions. He also won votes at a British general election despite being dead.

At the time of his death, Carroll was standing for election in the marginal constituency of Hampstead and Kilburn. If a candidate from a registered party dies the election has to be stopped and re-run, but if an independent candidate like Carroll dies the election goes ahead. Despite his declared ambition to be a candidate who secured no support and despite the significant drawback of being dead, he secured 113 votes, more than one of his living competitors managed. It was perhaps little consolation that a candidate who dies during an election has their deposit returned.

Elsewhere, dead candidates have been even more successful

than Mr Carroll. In the 2015 Myanmar election, the 54-year-old Soe Myint, a candidate for Aung San Suu Kyi's National League for Democracy Party, won, despite dying from a heart attack during the campaign. In the USA in 2018, the Republican candidate Dennis Hof, a dead brothel owner and reality TV star, won a local election in Nevada with 63 per cent of the vote, the latest in a line of American politicians elected despite their death.

The dead also vote. Votes from the dead can end up in the ballot box for a number of reasons: administrative error, mistaken identity, the death of people shortly after sending their postal ballots off, or as a result of deliberate fraud. In 2012 in Nassau County in New York, 270 votes from dead people were identified, including one man who had voted fourteen times since his death. In the 2013 Zimbabwe general election, the electoral registers were said to feature the names of two million dead people, including one record-breaking Methuselah aged 135; and in the most recent Zimbabwe election one person reportedly turned up to vote only to be told he was dead. In 2013 in Venezuela, there were reportedly more registered votes than there were people living in the country and it was claimed that 300,000 votes were cast in the names of dead people. In the USA, there could be as many as 1.8 million people on the electoral registers who are no longer alive and there have also been claims that dead people have been requesting ballot papers; President Trump has made unproven claims that voter fraud including dead people voting has influenced election outcomes.

In most cases, the votes of the dead are a result of the sheer administrative complexity of mass electoral registers and the challenge of keeping them up to date, meaning many dead people remain on registers for some time after their demise. In the UK, the electoral registers are estimated to be around 90 per cent accurate, so millions of voters are not correctly registered at their current address – including some who have died since the register was last updated.

Of the around 50 million population aged eighteen and over in the UK, approximately 550,000 people (roughly 1 per cent of the population) die each year. That's around 1,500 people per day – although there are seasonal variations, as well as spatial ones (life expectancy in Conservative-held seats is higher than in Labour-held ones, for example). The main electoral registration process closes around two weeks before polling day, though it closes nearer to polling day for those who request postal or proxy votes. Even if we assume the electoral register is fully accurate when it closes (which we know is not the case), around 21,500 potential voters could die between the closure of registration and polling day. Previously, this would not have been much of an issue. The dead might remain on the electoral register, and this might make them prime targets for those who wish to vote fraudulently, given that there is no risk of the real voter turning up and causing a scene. But this wasn't exactly a major concern.

The increasing use of postal voting, however, adds to the likelihood of dead people voting, because they may fill in their vote days before the election, then die before it is counted. In 2017, 8.4 million people requested postal votes, and these are much more likely to be cast than in-person votes. With the main postal voting registration closing around sixteen days before polling day and with the need to send a postal vote at least the day before polling day to ensure it arrives in time, around 3,000 potential postal

SEX, LIES AND POLITICS

votes could have been completed by voters who died before polling day. This is only an approximate figure. People who are about to die might be ill and less likely to vote, even by post. But on the other hand, postal voting request rates are disproportionately high among older people, and so the total number of deaths may well be higher. The true figure is impossible to know, but it is highly likely that hundreds, perhaps thousands, of votes counted at the last election were cast by the dead.

Could dead voters have determined the outcome in any constituency? The number of dead voters per constituency will be low. A figure of 3,000 across the country represents around five people per constituency. Even if we assume all of these people voted in one direction (unlikely), they will not have been numerous enough to determine the outcome in many constituencies. We can safely say that in 2015 Byron Davies, the successful Conservative candidate for Gower in Wales, who had the smallest majority – just twenty-seven votes – did not emerge victorious solely due to the votes of the dead (even though areas of south Wales have some of the lowest life expectancies and lowest healthy life expectancies in the UK). Similarly, the 2016 EU referendum was won by a wide enough margin – of over one million – that dead voters could not have swung it one way or the other. But in the 2017 general election, North East Fife was won by the SNP incumbent Stephen Gethins by a majority of just two votes. Such a small margin could easily have been determined by voters who had already died before the count began. Three other seats in 2017 were won with majorities of fewer than twenty-five votes.

With an ageing population (the population over eighty years old is projected to increase to eight million by 2050), higher turnout among older people, long-term inequalities in life expectancy across different areas and a growing use of postal votes, the chances are that even more constituencies' results will turn on the choices made by the recently departed.

FURTHER READING

Information on electoral registration regulations in the UK is available in 'Elections and Individual Electoral Registration' (Association of Electoral Administrators, 2015). For evidence of the quality of electoral registration and dead people being able to vote see *Election Initiatives* (Pew Trust, 2012). For information on the use of psychics to see how historical figures would have voted see Chippendale and Horrie's *Stick It up Your Punter! The Uncut Story of the Sun Newspaper* (Heinemann, 1990).

CHAPTER 39

When good neighbours don't become good friends: the extent of the Brexit divide

Maria Sobolewska

The British have a long tradition of judging their neighbours' behaviour and worrying what it might mean for the tone of the local area (and its house prices), as famously satirised by the twitching curtains of sitcom character Hyacinth Bucket. It turns out that people's Brexit choices have a big impact on how today's real-life Hyacinth Buckets view their potential neighbours.

In March 2018, YouGov fielded a survey to a nationally representative sample presenting respondents with two hypothetical families vying to move in next door. The descriptions of these families included nine different (randomly assigned) characteristics, from what kind of jobs they did and how many kids they had to where they went on holiday. Hidden among these other characteristics was how they had voted in the EU referendum. The experiment was designed like this not only to make it less obvious that it was interested in reactions to the Brexit vote but also to enable researchers to compare the effect of Brexit allegiances to other more usual factors that might affect social status, such as jobs, habits and origins. Respondents had to choose which of the two families they saw they would rather move in next door. To increase the statistical power, each respondent did this three times, looking overall at six different families; the percentage figures below average the effects of each individual characteristic across the different sets of combinations presented to people.

REMAINERS AND LEAVERS' PREFERENCES FOR A NEIGHBOUR

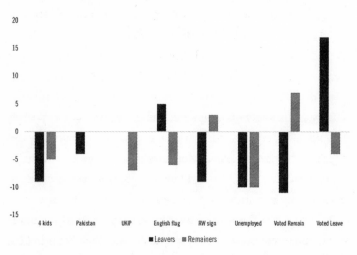

Note: the figure shows the average difference between the percentage of respondents who chose a family with this characteristic to move in next door over a family who did not have this characteristic. All of the differences shown are statistically significant.

In general, families where parents worked were preferred to those in which both parents were unemployed. Families with four – presumably loud – children were also seen as less desirable neighbours. Respondents liked neighbours who 'kept themselves to themselves' over those with other, perhaps more social, hobbies such as attending a local pub or running. Apart from unemployment, none of the other class indicators in the experiment (including the type of pub the family went to or where they preferred to holiday) had an impact on their perceived value as future neighbours, which, given the supposed obsession of the British with class, might be considered surprising.

Politics, by comparison, had a much larger effect.

The survey included three pieces of information about the new neighbour's politics: what they displayed in their window, how they voted in the 2016 referendum and which political party they voted for. They all mattered.

As the graph shows, both Leavers and Remainers preferred not to have a family who voted the opposite way in the 2016 referendum move in next door, but the size of this preference was larger among Leave voters. Leavers on average rewarded prospective new neighbours more if they also voted to Leave, and they also disliked the idea of Remain-voting neighbours more than Remainers disliked the idea of a Leave-supporting family moving in next door.

This could be because Leavers inherently dislike Remainers more than vice versa, but there may also be another factor in play. Negative discussion of Brexit in Remain-supporting media frequently focused on UKIP and the radical right, so Remain voters may focus on UKIP support more than Leave voting as a red-flag issue in a potential neighbour. By contrast, there was at the time of the survey no similarly divisive party on the Remain side. Because the experiment provided separate information about general election vote choices, Remain voters knew whether the prospective neighbour voted UKIP as well as Leave. Perhaps a Brexit voter who did not also vote UKIP, with all its potential connotations, did not seem as undesirable to our Remainers. UKIP support, however, was the second largest turn-off for Remain respondents – the only worse prospective neighbours in their minds were those where both parents were unemployed – so Remainers were indeed particularly opposed to UKIP voters. No other political party drew such a strong response from the Remainers.

Leave voters also penalised potential neighbours for displaying a Refugees Welcome sign in their window (as compared to a neutral 'no leafleting' sign) but looked favourably on the habit of displaying an English flag in a window. Leavers felt that a neighbour who was moving in from Pakistan was less desirable than neighbours who were moving from elsewhere in the UK, although the effect of this was small. Unlike Remain respondents, Leavers in our sample were not influenced by the party choices of their prospective neighbours.

For the Remainers in our sample, displaying an English flag was an undesirable characteristic in their prospective neighbours, suggesting they sympathise with Emily Thornberry's negative reaction to such displays on the campaign trail in 2014, a reaction which got her sacked from the shadow Cabinet. Conversely, Remainers liked their new neighbours to have a Refugees Welcome sign in their window and, unlike Leavers, Remainers did not care about the national origins of their potential future neighbours.

Several other studies have similarly found that the Brexit vote is part of a broader cultural divide, in which Leave and Remain voters hold strong stereotypes about their opponents and in which there are strong linkages between the economic and social prospects of neighbourhoods and their Brexit vote choices (as discussed, for example, in Chapter 45).

It is often said that polite conversation should not include such topics as politics and money, and Brexit politics conforms to this rule. You should perhaps refrain from sharing your Brexit preference with your future neighbours if you want to make friends, unless you are sure that they have voted the way you have. Given that more people voted to Leave, and these people seem to feel more strongly about their Brexit identity, this is especially valuable advice for those who voted to stay in the EU in June 2016.

FURTHER READING

For classic reads on how political attachments form the basis of social identification, which dictates what we think of and how we interact with other people, see either 'Partisanship as Social Identity; Implications for the Study of Party Polarization' by Shanto Iyengar and Masha Krupenkin (*The Forum*, 2018) or *Partisan hearts and minds: Political parties and the social identities of voters* by Donald Green et al. (Yale University Press, 2004). For research into how a Brexit identity is developing see 'Divided by the Vote: Affective Polarization in the Wake of Brexit' by Sara Hobolt et al. (2018).

CHAPTER 40

Areal interpolation: or how we know how constituencies voted in the 2016 referendum

Chris Hanretty

The 2016 referendum on the UK's membership of the European Union was counted in 382 different 'counting areas'. In England, Wales and Scotland, these counting areas followed the boundaries of local authorities, which is normal practice in British referendums.

Yet, save in rare cases, Westminster constituencies don't cover the same areas as local authorities. Anyone who wanted to know how each Westminster constituency voted in the referendum needed a way to take local authority results and 're-map' them on to Westminster boundaries. This is a technical problem (geographers call it 'areal interpolation'), but it's also a political problem. It's much harder for an MP to respect the wishes of a majority of their constituents if they don't know how a majority voted.

The starting point for remapping referendum results is the strong association between demographics and voting. Although we might not know much about how areas voted, we do know a lot about how different types of people voted and we know which types of people live in which constituencies. For example, there was a strong relationship between someone's education and age and the way they voted in the referendum (as discussed in Chapter 47), and we know a lot about how different constituencies vary in terms of their voters' ages and education levels.

These associations mean we can form reasonable guesses about how different areas voted just on the basis of their demographic profile, in the same way that we can make reasonable guesses about how individuals vote on the basis of which newspaper they read (if any). We can estimate a statistical model, which tries to 'predict' how each area votes as a function of different predictors, including not just the proportion of people with different types of educational qualifications but also things like average age, home-ownership and class.

Thanks to the Census, we can make predictions at a very local level. Census output areas are small tracts which have populations of between 100 and 625 individuals. Because the Census reports demographic profiles for these areas, we can predict how each output area voted.

These predictions, on their own, are likely to be both creepy and wrong. They'll be creepy because even electoral obsessives are likely to find it odd to see predictions for individual streets or tower blocks. They'll be wrong because any model is a simplification of reality. But the beautiful thing about these very fine-grained predictions for output areas is that we can add them up to get pretty reliable predictions for either local authority areas or Westminster constituencies.

Because we know which output areas go in which local authorities, and which output areas go in which Westminster constituencies, making predictions for output areas allows us to produce estimates for either type of area. You can make predictions for output areas, go through each local authority area, scaling up or down the predictions for all of the output areas so as to match the known local authority outcome, and then add up all of the scaled predictions to give a figure for each constituency.

How good are the estimates this produces? In the six months following the referendum, two BBC journalists painstakingly assembled ward-level results from all those local returning officers who had been savvy enough to keep ward-level ballots separate. These figures are the best figures we have, although even they aren't perfect (they don't take account of postal votes, for example).

Still, this research allows us to work out how well these estimates matched the known figures for around 113 seats. The estimates didn't over- or underestimate the Leave share of the vote in each area. For two-fifths of the seats, the true figure was within 1 percentage point of the estimate; for three-fifths, within 2 percentage points. That's not perfect, but it's about as close as we're going to get. From these estimates, we can learn some useful things.

First, although the referendum nationally was close, Leave won far more constituencies than did Remain. According to the estimates, 410 of 650 seats (63 per cent) voted to Leave. That's lower than it could have been: in theory, Leave could have won 100 per cent of the seats if it had won 52 per cent in each and every constituency. But that figure still sets up a problem for parliamentary representation. If each MP blindly followed the wishes of a majority of their constituents, then 63 per cent of Parliament would be in favour of Brexit. That's a greater figure than in the country as a whole. You may think that's a welcome corrective, given that before the referendum a majority of MPs were in favour of remaining in the European Union. Yet it would still leave the 48 per cent disappointed.

Second, seats represented by Conservative and Labour MPs disproportionately voted Leave. If we go back to the seats as they were in 2015, then 148 of 232 Labour seats (64 per cent) voted Leave. That proportion is lower than the same figure for the Conservatives (75 per cent), but it is more politically damaging for Labour. It may seem paradoxical, but the areas represented by Labour MPs voted (sometimes heavily) to Leave even though the people who voted for Labour MPs generally voted to Remain. The tensions between 'representing my area' and 'representing those who voted for me' are clearest for Labour MPs.

Third, in the 2017 election, the Conservatives did best in seats that had voted to Leave. For every 1 percentage point increase in the Leave vote share, the Conservative share of the vote increased by one-quarter of a percentage point.

Figures on how each constituency voted in the referendum are quite simple political facts. They have, however, made life very complicated for MPs. For most issues, most of the time, MPs can make claims about what their constituents think without any risk of being told they're wrong. Now MPs have a clear indication of what their constituents think – or rather, what they thought at a particular point in time in response to a particular question. Few people (and almost no MPs) would claim that MPs should simply follow constituency opinion on every issue. That would leave no role for party policy or for individual judgement. Many MPs will be happy defending their individual judgement and their party's policies. But I suspect that MPs would have had an easier life if voting figures for Westminster constituencies had never surfaced.

FURTHER READING

For a full description of how estimates of referendum votes by constituency were produced see 'Areal interpolation and the UK's referendum on EU membership' by Chris Hanretty (*Journal of Elections, Public Opinion and Parties*, 2017). Ward-level figures for selected wards are available from Martin Rosenbaum's 'Local voting figures shed new light on EU referendum' (BBC News, February 2017). The strong relationship between demographic characteristics and the referendum vote (at the local authority level) is well described in 'The 2016 referendum, Brexit and the left behind: An aggregate-level analysis of the result' by Matthew Goodwin and Oliver Heath (*Political Quarterly*, 2016).

*'It is the folly of too many to mistake the echo
of a London coffee-house for the voice
of the kingdom.'*

— JONATHAN SWIFT

—CHAPTER 41—

The people are perceptive: immigration and the EU

Geoffrey Evans

The public are often thought to be relatively ignorant about social and political issues. Even when true, this can be a little unfair. The complexity and (at times deliberate) ambiguity of many issues, and the ways they are 'spun' by the parties – keen not to be on the wrong side of a debate – often make it hard for voters to make sense of things. But there is one issue where the public did put two and two together: immigration and the EU. Actual immigration rates are the key to understanding the public's level of concern about immigration, but it's not just about the level of immigration *per se* – it's also about where people are coming from. The rise of immigration from EU accession countries after 2004 led to a train of events that were to have unparalleled political consequences.

Immigration increased markedly at the end of the last century and has remained exceptionally high since. Public concern about immigration has closely tracked this rise in numbers. The share naming immigration as the most important issue on the political agenda rose from under 5 per cent in the mid-1990s to nearly 35 per cent in the mid-2000s. There was a dip following the onset of the economic crisis in 2007–08 – unsurprising given the magnitude of the crisis – but rising anxiety about immigration resumed soon after as the economy recovered, and by the time of the 2016 EU referendum had reached the highest levels on record, with 40 per cent or more naming it as the nation's most pressing issue.

In the past, the overall rate of immigration had no implications for attitudes towards the EU – as most immigrants didn't come from other European countries. In 1975, concern about immigration was high, but it had no consequence for the vote to stay in the Common Market: anti-immigration voters decided overwhelmingly to stay in Europe. But this changed radically. Evidence separating Commonwealth, EU and 'other' sources of immigration in the years leading up to the 2016 referendum shows that the EU loomed far larger in the immigration statistics than it used to. Estimates of international migration provided by the International Passenger Survey show that EU immigration played no part in the rise in immigration before 2004 – this was produced by an increase in asylum seekers, students and workers from other parts of the world. EU immigration only took off with the 2004 accession of former communist-bloc countries of Eastern Europe into the EU, and the government's decision not to restrict immigration from these countries during the first five years of EU membership. Thereafter, EU immigration formed a major component of immigration into Britain. By 2013, it was by far the largest component, and continuing to grow as migrants from crisis-hit Eurozone countries sought better opportunities in Britain.

If we compare these trends in immigration from different sources with trends in concern about immigration expressed via responses to questions about what people think are 'the most important issues facing the country' obtained from polls conducted by Ipsos MORI, we find that concern about immigration closely tracks the surge in EU immigration but not immigration from other sources, which was flat or falling in the years following Prime Minister David Cameron's stated (and doomed) intention to reduce immigration to less than 100,000 per year.

In itself, however, this aggregate relationship isn't compelling evidence that individual voters were linking their attitudes to immigration with their views about the EU. We need to look at how individual voters think about the two issues. This can be examined using a long series of monthly surveys (the Continuous Monitoring Surveys), which each month asked British voters for their views on both immigration and the EU. Using this data, we can see how the link between immigration and the EU in individual voters' minds changed over time. The figure below shows the difference in EU approval scores ('How much do you approve of Britain's membership of the EU?') between respondents who believe immigration is one of the most important issues facing the country, and those who don't. Each black dot represents the size of the difference in approval of the EU between people who think immigration is one of the most important issues facing the country and those who don't. The middle line is the best estimate of the position of the changing slope over time. The grey area of the graph represents the width of the confidence interval, indicating a 95 per cent probability that the true score lies within this area.

RELATIONSHIP BETWEEN APPROVAL OF THE EU AND
CONCERN ABOUT IMMIGRATION, 2004–13

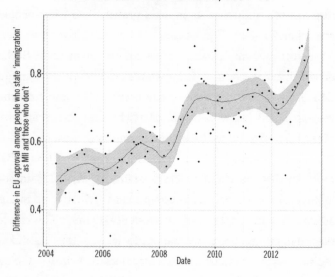

The difference in EU approval between people who believe immigration is 'an important problem' and those who do not increases during the years following the 2004 opening of the EU to accession countries from Eastern Europe before flattening off from 2009 to 2011 during the economic crisis, only to rise steeply again after 2012, as EU immigration rates also shot upwards. In less than a decade of the 2004 accession to the EU, concern about immigration went from being moderately distinct from approval of the EU to being strongly linked in the mind of the public.

This had a major influence on the EU referendum vote. The British Election Survey found that only 10 per cent of people who did *not* believe too many immigrants have been let into the country would vote to leave the EU. But no less than 50 per cent of those who believed too many immigrants have been let in would do so. When asked to explain in their own words why they voted Leave in the 2016 referendum, immigration dominated people's responses.

Since the referendum, however, immigration from the EU has declined: between June 2016 and June 2018, overall net immigration dropped from 336,000 to 273,000, with net immigration from the so-called EU8 accession countries, which includes Poland and the Czech Republic, falling by 66 per cent over the same period. With falling immigration comes falling concern: Ipsos MORI found that 48 per cent of people rated immigration as an important issue in June 2016, but only 20 per cent did so two years later. Much will depend on whether a Brexit deal that includes restriction of freedom of movement is finally implemented. Should it not be, and if EU citizens still see Britain as a desirable destination, then there remains the possibility that immigration will rise again, and concern about immigration will re-emerge. The issue still has the potential to shape British politics.

FURTHER READING

For a more detailed analysis of the issues raised here see Geoff Evans and Jon Mellon's 'Immigration, Euroscepticism, and the Rise and Fall of UKIP' (*Party Politics*, 2019). For a study of the sources and political implications of immigration and Euroscepticism in Britain see Robert Ford and Matthew Goodwin's *Revolt on the Right: Explaining Support for the Radical Right in Britain* (Routledge, 2014) and for an accessible analysis of why immigration featured so strongly in the EU referendum and the politics that followed see Geoff Evans and Anand Menon's *Brexit and British Politics* (Polity, 2017).

—CHAPTER 42—

'The Eastern Europeans are taking all the Asian jobs': ethnic minority support for Brexit

Neema Begum

I t is a common observation that the vote for Brexit in 2016 was driven, at least in part, by racism; as the novelist Will Self claimed, 'Not all Brexiters are racists, but almost all racists will be voting for Brexit.' Of all voters, the one group that we might have expected to be most sensitive to this would be Britain's ethnic minority voters. While a majority of BAME voters did indeed vote Remain, almost a third (29 per cent) backed Leave. The Brexit campaign secured more ethnic minority support than the Conservatives had managed in decades – and not for want of trying – and roughly fifteen times the level of ethnic minority support the main anti-EU party, UKIP, ever achieved.

Why would black and Asian people, who are often the targets of racism and more likely to be in favour of immigration, support what many saw as an anti-immigrant, even racist, campaign?

Interviews and focus groups carried out after the referendum reveal that these ethnic minority Leave voters often had similar concerns to the population at large: they felt that the EU was encroaching on UK sovereignty, overriding UK laws and imposing excessive red tape. BAME Leavers were more likely to be male, older and foreign-born, and less likely to have taken advantage of the ability to travel, live or work in EU countries.

However, there was one crucial difference: compared to white Leave voters, BAME Brexiters were also resentful of the relative ease of access they perceived Eastern Europeans as having to live and work in the UK compared to other immigrants. This stood in stark contrast to the situation many minority voters, usually Commonwealth migrants, faced when trying to bring their own relatives to Britain or recruit staff from outside the EU. Campaign groups such as Muslims for Britain and Africans for Britain were formed in the run-up to the referendum and argued that it was unfair that EU citizens could so easily come to the UK while established Commonwealth migrant communities – from countries with long-standing historical links to Britain – and the descendants of migrants who helped to rebuild Britain after war with its European neighbours faced much greater difficulties with the migration system.

Despite the presence of such campaign groups, it was British Indians and black Caribbeans who were the most pro-Brexit according to Understanding Society data, with 33 per cent and 34 per cent supporting Leave respectively. Older black Caribbean interviewees spoke of the difficulty former British colonies in the Caribbean had in exporting crops to the UK due to EU trade rules.

The marginally less pro-Brexit ethnic minority groups, including Bangladeshis and Pakistanis, picked up on Islamophobia during the campaign, including the oft-asserted claim that Turkey's entry into the EU was imminent and the fears around a majority-Muslim country potentially having 'open-door' access to the UK through freedom of movement.

Many of the BAME Brexiters from all backgrounds associated Eastern Europeans with crime going up, fraudulent benefit claims and a strain on the NHS, school places and other public services – attitudes pretty similar to those found among white Leave voters. But, as well as this, Eastern Europeans were said to be a threat to the availability of jobs which are usually low-paid and filled by working-class ethnic minorities. As one Leave voter told me, 'The Eastern Europeans are taking all the Asian jobs. Corner shops, taxis, kebab shops and restaurants.' The referendum therefore revealed tensions between longer-settled BAME groups and newer Eastern European arrivals. Many ethnic minorities saw Brexit as an opportunity to put a stop to Eastern European immigration, which, like white voters, they saw as disruptive and threatening.

And while some BAME Leave voters were indeed concerned with racism, they were worried not only about homegrown racism but also about the intolerance EU migrants may bring with them from Europe. They felt that other EU countries may be more racist or Islamophobic, especially as overtly racist radical right-wing parties are much more successful in many European countries than in the UK. BAME Leave voters felt that the UK was less racist than most European countries, a place where minority rights are better protected and where hijab bans, for example, would be unthinkable, whereas 'Europe' was conceived of by some as a 'white fortress', permitting white immigration while obstructing the entry of non-whites.

Some of my interviewees saw evidence of this in the EU's response to the refugee crisis. There was also criticism of specific EU policies such as the Common Agricultural Policy, which were seen as disadvantaging developing economies in Africa and Asia such as those that they or their parents originated in. Leaving the EU, it was felt, would increase trade and migration between the UK and the Commonwealth.

Reporting in Leicester during the campaign, the journalist Robert Peston said that he 'assumed it was a collective wind-up when almost every Asian I met said to me that they would be voting for Brexit'. It was not. Although the majority voted Remain, ethnic minority support for Brexit was constantly underestimated. Some of this reflected real resentments arising from differences in EU and non-EU migration rules, reinforced by BAME voters' belief that it is their countries, not the EU, that should have a privileged relationship with Britain. But commentators also underestimated how anti-immigration messages could appeal to immigrants or their children, with the targets of xenophobia in earlier periods now adopting similar stereotypes and hostility with regards to newer arrivals. Ethnic minority support for Brexit is part of a wider phenomenon of immigrant or minority groups voting for anti-immigration campaigns and parties, including Latinos for Trump and ethnic minorities voting for the Freedom Party in the Netherlands. It can be surprisingly easy for people to close the door on others once they have passed through it themselves.

FURTHER READING

For more on contemporary trends in ethnic minority political attitudes and party support see 'Ethnic Minorities at the 2017 British General Election' by Nicole Martin and Omar Khan (Runnymede Trust Briefing, 2019). There is also increasing scholarship on race and the EU referendum, including '"Post-race" racisms in the narratives of "Brexit" voters' (*The Sociological Review*, 2019) by Tina G. Patel and Laura Connelly. For an analysis of ethnic minority voting patterns in the EU referendum see 'Left Out of the Left Behind: Ethnic Minority Support for Brexit' by Nicole Martin et al. (Social Science Research Network, 2019).

CHAPTER 43

What would Margaret do? How we project our views onto others

Philip Cowley

Towards the end of the Brexit referendum campaign in 2016, YouGov polled the British public to ask them how they thought a range of thirty fictional characters would be voting. If you calculated a net pro-Remain score (the percentage thinking that person would back Remain minus the percentage thinking they'd vote Leave), you had a list topped by Geraldine Granger, the Vicar of Dibley, who was seen as the most pro-Remain (+21), and which ended with the most pro-Leave, Jim Royle, from *The Royle Family* (-38).

It's easy to mock this sort of thing, and plenty did at the time: 'pointless', 'polling jumping the shark' and so on. Some even thought pollsters asked daft questions like this just to generate cheap headlines. What a cynical world we live in. Yet answers to questions like this can tell you quite a lot, both about the specific issue – in this case, the referendum campaign – and about voters in general.

For one thing, the poll did seem to show a divide in how people saw supporters of Remain and Leave. On the Remain side, as well as the Vicar of Dibley, there was Mary Poppins (+13), Miranda (+11) and Doctor Who (+9), while backing Leave there was Hyacinth Bucket (-13), Tracy Barlow (-15), Del Boy (-28) and Basil Fawlty (-36).

Obviously, there's some subjective judgement in how we view these characters, but broadly speaking those who were thought to be likely to support Remain seemed nice, if perhaps a bit smug or sanctimonious, while on the Leave side there were more rogues and chancers – some loveable, some not.

This sort of insight is one of the reasons polling companies like left-field questions. Perhaps the most famous is the Tin Man and Scarecrow question first asked by John Zogby in the 2000 US election. 'You live in the land of Oz,' Zogby asked his respondents, 'and the candidates are the Tin Man, who's all brains and no heart, and the Scarecrow, who's all heart and no brains. Who would you vote for?' Zogby claimed it allowed him to see what voters wanted, freed from their perceptions of individual candidates or parties.

It's also why participants in focus groups are often asked to visualise the political parties as biscuits or cars or animals – because this can often get at something that more conventional questions might miss. Sure, they also generate easy publicity for the polling company, but that's not an inherently bad thing: you can generate cheap headlines and still be interesting.

But there are two important caveats, which also tell us a lot about voters and how they engage with questions like this. First, when you look at the full data tables, rather than just the headlines, you often find that the numbers saying 'Don't know' to these sorts of questions are really substantial – in this particular case as high as 55 per cent for both Tracy Barlow and Arthur Dent – either because respondents don't know who the characters are or because they don't really have a view on their politics. The lowest 'Don't know' scores in this survey were for Basil Fawlty and Del Boy, but even these were still 34 per cent. For twenty-six out of the thirty characters, the plurality response was 'Don't know'. In other words, the data didn't really show that the public thought Captain Birdseye (-11) was a Leaver; when half of all respondents said they didn't know, the data actually showed that the public didn't really have a clue what Captain Birdseye thought about Brexit.

More importantly, second, when you look at the cross-breaks, it becomes clear how much of the aggregate score is being driven by people's own partisan views. Take James Bond, for example. He was seen as pro-Brexit (-22) by Brexit supporters and pro-Remain (+30) by Remain voters. His overall score (+5) was merely the product of these two very different views. The same sort of split applied to Doctor Who, Postman Pat, Sherlock Holmes, Miranda and so on.

And for those respondents who didn't know how they were going to vote in the referendum, the 'Don't knows' about fictional characters became even more significant, rising to a massive 77 per cent for Arthur Dent, because those who lack a partisan view of their own about the referendum struggle to project any view onto these fictional characters. They lacked, in the jargon, a heuristic enabling them to answer the question. Which in turn tells you a great deal about how many partisans answered the questions.

In fact, of the thirty characters YouGov polled about in 2016, there were just eleven where respondents from both sides of the

Brexit debate agreed – and these eleven excluded almost all of the broadly positive characters.

For the record, there were ten characters where both Remain and Leave voters agreed would be for Brexit: Alan Partridge, Jim Royle, Del Boy, Hyacinth Bucket, Pat Butcher, Tracy Barlow, Captain Mainwaring, Catherine Tate's Nan, Cruella de Vil and Basil Fawlty. It must say something that even Leavers thought Cruella De Vil would be one of theirs.

Mind you, the only pro-Remain character that both sides agreed on was Sir Humphrey Appleby, the scheming bureaucrat from *Yes, Minister* and *Yes, Prime Minister*, which isn't great for Remainers either.

YouGov repeated the exercise in 2017 for the general election. The most likely to vote Conservative was Sir Humphrey Appleby; for Labour it was Jim Royle. (Combining the two surveys, this makes Appleby a Conservative Remainer and Royle a Labour Leaver, both minority positions in their parties.) Groundskeeper Willie from *The Simpsons* was the most likely to vote SNP, and Doctor Who the most likely to vote Green, with Bridget Jones the most likely to back the Lib Dems. But, again, there were masses of 'Don't knows' – in twenty-one cases, 'Don't know' was the plurality response – along with plenty of partisan answering.

And in 2019 the pollsters asked a similar question, but this time about how people thought Margaret Thatcher would have voted on Brexit. Thatcher was certainly not imaginary, although by the time of the referendum she had been dead for three years. You will probably be able to guess what happened. Remainers thought she'd be a Remainer (by 42 per cent to 25 per cent), while Leavers thought she'd be a Leaver (48 per cent to 18 per cent). And of those who rated Thatcher highly, thinking she was a 'good' or a 'great' Prime Minister, and who therefore might want to pray her in aid, the difference was even starker. Pro-Thatcher Remainers thought she would have voted Remain by 62 per cent to 17 per cent, while pro-Thatcher Leavers thought she would have voted Leave by 60 per cent to 17 per cent. Whether they are imaginary or dead, we are happy to project our views onto others.

FURTHER READING

The original report is in 'Brexit Basil and Bremain Bridget' by Chris Curtis (YouGov, 2016). The 2017 follow-up ('How British fictional characters might vote: 2017 general election edition') and the polling on Margaret Thatcher ('Margaret Thatcher: the public view forty years on') were both by Matthew Smith for YouGov. Zogby's question is explained in his *The Way We'll Be* (Random House, 2008). *Pay Me Forty Quid and I'll Tell You* by Michael Ashcroft and Kevin Culwick (Biteback, 2015) contains fascinating focus group reports on the 2015 election, including how voters saw David Cameron as a fox, Nigel Farage as a weasel, and Ed Miliband as 'one of those animals that, when you go to the zoo, you're not bothered whether you see it or not'.

—CHAPTER 44—

It's all relative: why it matters who is doing better than whom

Jane Green

The Brexit map looks clear enough. Metropolitan areas were more likely to vote Remain, whereas rural and coastal parts of the country were more likely to vote Leave. Globalisation, it is argued, created clear 'winners' and 'losers', and successive governments failed sufficiently to compensate for these economic inequalities. This, combined with a period of austerity, fuelled the vote for Brexit and led to sharp geographic polarisation in attitudes towards Brexit.

But most survey-based studies find little such effect. Rather, they find that attitudes towards immigration outweigh various kinds of economic factors in explaining the vote, which suggests that any aggregate economic relationships might simply be picking up the kinds of demographic factors that tend to make people more pro- or anti-immigration. On this reading, the vote for Brexit was based on a cultural backlash rather than economic discontent.

Yet what if economics needs to be thought about differently? What if people care about how they are doing relative to others, rather than how they are doing in the absolute or how they think the national economy is doing? In order to try to resolve these two different interpretations, the British Election Study tried a different way to measure economic attitudes. Rather than asking people about how things have gone for them as individuals, and for the country as a whole, it asked them how they thought different groups in society had been doing over the previous year.

The graph below shows how Leave and Remain voters thought white British people and ethnic minorities had been doing over the previous year. The bars are the differences between the percentages saying a group had done better and the percentages saying a group had done worse. The sample is white British respondents. Negative scores mean that, on average, more respondents thought the group had done badly economically over the past year than thought it was doing well.

Remain and Leave voters had very different views about how things had gone. Remain voters thought both white and ethnic minority groups had had a bad year economically, but that ethnic minorities had faced worse economic struggles than white voters. Leave voters also thought it had been a bad year economically for the white British, but they thought the economy had done better for ethnic minorities.

These relative group judgements mattered. When white British respondents thought ethnic minority immigrants were doing much better economically, they were over a fifth more likely to vote for Brexit. This effect is even stronger for white respondents who thought ethnic minority immigrants were doing better than white British people. While Brexit choices were not linked to individual economic circumstances, they were linked to group economic circumstances, and in particular to how people thought their group was getting on relative to others.

VIEWS OF RELATIVE ECONOMIC SUCCESS, BY BREXIT VOTE

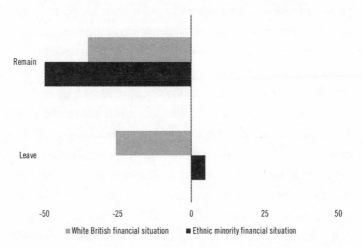

Beliefs about relative economic winners and losers are not just confined to race; they apply to geography too. There's similar evidence that resentments directed towards the capital mattered: when respondents thought Londoners were doing better than people living in their own community, they were also more likely to vote to leave the EU, although the effect is smaller than for the group comparisons based on race.

These findings are consistent with a view that people don't just care about how they do, they also care about how other groups, particularly groups they see as rivals, are doing. What matters is who people think is getting ahead. In particular, thinking rival groups are getting ahead while they are left out is a politically potent mix. Viewed through this lens, economic evaluations did indeed have a big impact on Brexit vote choices, even after controlling for any negative feelings some voters have towards groups such as immigrants in general. It's not a matter of cultural resentment or economic inequalities: for many voters, Brexit choices emerged from how the two sentiments mixed together.

These kinds of group-based tensions and anxieties can have effects in other ways. For example, views of immigration are often less about how voters are individually affected by migrants and more about the threats they think migrants may pose to the group they belong to. Group-based economic resentments could also help resolve an ongoing debate in America about whether Donald Trump's presidential victory was the product of economic or racial resentments. There, too, researchers have noted both that Trump did better in deprived towns and rural areas and, when we study Trump voters individually, that their views about migrants, minorities and women seem more important than their economic circumstances. However, here, as with our Brexit example, it may be misleading to treat these economic and racial resentments as separate and competing explanations. Voters whose areas experience long-term economic decline and worsening job prospects may turn against migrants whom they see as getting ahead when their group is falling behind. For these reasons, and using our group-based findings of economic winners and losers on vote choices for Brexit, it is probably much too soon to claim that Brexit, or Trump for that matter, were a matter of culture not economics. For many voters, those two things go together.

FURTHER READING

For analysis of global import shocks and Brexit see Italo Colantone and Piero Stanig's 'Global competition and Brexit' (*American Political Science Review*, 2018). For the link between long-term economics, immigration attitudes and Brexit see 'Long-Term Economic Distress, Cultural Backlash, and Support for Brexit' by Miguel Carreras et al. (*Comparative Political Studies*, 2019). More details of the study reported here can be found in 'Who Gets What: The Group-Based Economic Vote for Brexit' by Jane Green et al. (forthcoming paper).

—CHAPTER 45—

Location, location, location? Brexit and the predictive power of house prices

Ben Ansell

Over the past few decades, the UK has seen an unprecedented boom in housing prices, but one that has been very unevenly distributed, with London and the south-east the chief beneficiaries. Concerns abound that house prices are reinforcing geographical inequalities in Britain by making internal migration difficult, thus locking in advantage and disadvantage across regions. The British housing market also makes inequality worse because for many it acts as a substitute for the welfare state, with individuals relying on their housing wealth to help provide for retirement and insure against labour market shocks.

So, housing is important in economic terms. But it also matters politically, for two main reasons. First, since people can choose where to live – within reason – they often sort into like-minded areas. And this tendency can be reinforced by a second effect: the tendency of the local environment to influence how people perceive the world. If you feel that people in your local community are never listened to, it's not surprising you might be suspicious of national and supranational authority – both of Westminster and of Brussels. If people in your area are struggling with unemployment and stagnant wages, you may feel the economic status quo is not working, whatever is happening in other, perhaps booming, regions. And if people around you all express similar opinions about political matters – say, the merits of Brexit – that is likely to reinforce your convictions.

Owning a house amplifies these effects. Houses are geographically fixed – save for owners of mobile homes, you cannot move your house with you across the country – and the housing market is quite illiquid – it is costly and laborious to move house, so people do it rarely. Plus, house prices vary dramatically across the country, so you might not be able to afford to move. Houses lock people into their local communities, for good and for ill. And that means that how a local community is faring will have particularly strong effects on homeowners, who are literally and figuratively invested in such communities.

Given all of this, it should come as no surprise to discover that there was a relationship between that perennial British obsession – house prices – and the Brexit vote. While people voted to Remain or Leave the European Union for a range of reasons, one important factor was how they felt their communities had fared over the past few decades of EU membership. Those communities that were falling behind economically appear to have been those, on the whole, where support for Leave was strongest. And house prices give us a sense of this effect – one way of thinking of house prices is as the price people are willing to pay to join a community. House prices are thus a great indicator of exactly how much people value various locations as places to live. Such prices turn out to be stronger predictors of support for or opposition to Brexit than other local economic indicators such as unemployment and average wages.

The graph demonstrates the relationship between support for Remain and average house prices in each local authority in England and Wales. The size of the bubbles in the figure reflects the population of each local authority.

HOUSE PRICES AND SUPPORT FOR REMAIN AT THE LOCAL AUTHORITY LEVEL IN ENGLAND AND WALES

Note: This figure shows the relationship between house prices and the percentage of the EU referendum vote for Remain. The size of the bubbles reflects the population of the electorate. House prices are logged in order to compress areas with very high prices.

There was a very strong positive relationship between house prices in a local authority and support for Remain. Areas with median house prices of around £100,000 in 2015 averaged a 30 per cent Remain to 70 per cent Leave split, whereas those with median prices above £500,000 averaged the reverse: 70 per cent Remain to 30 per cent Leave.

Some indicative local authorities have been labelled on the figure. House prices alone explain around half of the variation across local authorities in the Brexit vote. But whereas most fit pretty closely to the line, we do see some outliers – Liverpool, Manchester, Bristol and Oxford were all more pro-Remain than predicted by house prices and Boston, Medway and Havering more pro-Leave. So prices alone do not explain everything. Still, the overall pattern is strong, and, importantly, it remains if we add statistical controls for unemployment, income, ethnic composition and age profile. And the pattern holds up within local authorities (if we compare wards where we have data) and is strongest among homeowners: the people who are the most locked into how their community is faring.

House prices map on to Brexit voting much more strongly than they do on to traditional Labour/Conservative voting, highlighting how the divide exposed by Brexit creates problems for both parties. It's not surprising that both parties are torn, with many Labour MPs in areas with cheaper housing worried about keeping hold of Leave voters, and Tory MPs in leafy south-eastern suburbs concerned about angry Remainers. It also highlights one of the consequences of the 2010–15 coalition's choice to engage in fiscal austerity, relying on the Bank of England to engage in unprecedented monetary stimulus. This led to a second housing boom as the south-east shot away from the rest of the country again, even as wages flatlined and public spending collapsed elsewhere.

Wealthy, traditionally Conservative areas saw large increases in house prices, which in turn underpinned support for Remain. In the meantime, poorer, traditionally Labour areas had stagnant housing markets, reinforcing community support for leaving the European Union. This further polarised Britain's economic geography, mirrored by its unequal housing market, and set the scene for a new and chaotic form of polarisation from 2016 onwards.

FURTHER READING

The links between house prices and voting are analysed in 'Housing and Populism' (*West European Politics*, 2019) by David Adler and Ben Ansell and 'The Politics of Housing' (*Annual Review of Political Science*, 2019) by Ben Ansell. For a broader analysis of the geographic polarisation discussed here see 'The divergent dynamics of cities and towns: Geographical polarisation after Brexit' by Will Jennings and Gerry Stoker *(Political Quarterly*, 2019). A good general overview of the politics of housing in the UK is *All That Is Solid: The Great Housing Disaster* by Danny Dorling (Penguin, 2015).

—CHAPTER 46—

Feeling hard done by: perceptions of gender and ethnic discrimination and the Brexit vote

Rosalind Shorrocks

We are living in an age of ever-increasing support for gender and racial equality. As recently as 1984, 43 per cent of survey respondents agreed that it was a man's job to earn money and a woman's job to look after the home and family. By 2017, that number had fallen to 8 per cent. And, as discussed in Chapter 30, 60 per cent of white people in the early 1980s said they would mind if a close relative married someone who was black, but by 2013 this figure had dropped to 20 per cent.

Increasing gender and racial equality is usually thought of in terms of correcting the historical disadvantages faced by women and ethnic minorities. But not everyone sees it that way. British Election Study (BES) questions fielded in 2016 found that between 15 and 20 per cent of people think there is discrimination against men, in favour of women. Around 20 per cent think that there is discrimination against white people and in favour of black and Asian people. Such views were particularly prevalent among older white voters. Older men are especially likely to perceive discrimination against men, while younger women are especially likely to perceive discrimination against women and black and Asian people.

Such views matter politically. In the case of Brexit, the belief that men are now the gender facing discrimination predicts support for leaving the European Union, even after accounting for other factors. A similar effect occurs with regards to ethnicity: while most people think of racial discrimination as hurting the prospects of ethnic minorities, those who believe it is white British people who now face discrimination were also more likely to support Brexit. The graph below illustrates this point: the probability of voting Leave, shown on the y-axis, was highest for men who perceived discrimination against men. The left side of the graph also shows, however, that perceiving discrimination in favour of or against men didn't matter for women's Leave vote, as the line for women is flat. The right side shows that both (white) men and women who perceived discrimination against white British people had a higher probability of voting Leave than those who perceived discrimination in favour of this group, with the steep line on this side of the graph indicating a strong relationship between perceiving such discrimination and voting to leave the EU.

This is part of a broader phenomenon sometimes described as a 'cultural backlash'. Some have argued that communities that have seen industrial decline – and white working-class men within these communities in particular – are resentful at changes in society they believe have benefited other groups at their expense, including immigrants and ethnic minorities. A related perception is that women have received unfair advantages at the expense of working men, as women have entered the labour force in larger numbers at the same time as economic prospects for working-class men have declined, relatively speaking. The data from the BES indicate that a small section of the population in the UK does indeed think like this, and it influences their politics.

THE RELATIONSHIP BETWEEN PERCEPTIONS OF DISCRIMINATION AND THE PROBABILITY OF VOTING TO LEAVE THE EU

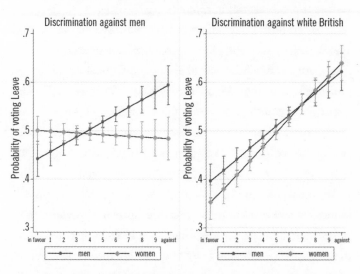

Note: The figure shows predicted probabilities calculated from logistic regression models for Leave voting among white voters, controlling for gender, age, income, education, authoritarian–libertarian values, attitudes towards immigrants, and British identity.

In the US, too, gender and racial resentment have become politically consequential. Thinking that women are unfairly advantaged and men disadvantaged made voters more likely to vote for Donald Trump in 2016, even when taking into account other factors.

Resentment towards black people played a role in the election of Republican candidates prior to 2016, but the effect was stronger when it came to Donald Trump. It would seem, then, that white men who feel they are losing out to women and minorities are mobilising behind campaigns attacking a status quo which they feel is unfair to them. Those who felt unfairly disadvantaged by being white and male seem to have been attracted by campaigns focused on restoring the past order of things. 'Take Back Control' or 'Make America Great Again' are resonant messages if you feel your group has lost out in recent years.

Issues around gender and race have remained on the political agenda since 2016. The #MeToo movement reached Westminster in 2017, with allegations of sexual harassment made against numerous politicians. Mandatory gender pay gap reporting and the centenary of the extension of the franchise to some women in 2018 produced extensive coverage of women's political disadvantage both historically and in present-day Britain. At the same time, the Windrush scandal highlighted the negative impact of government policy on legal migrant groups, and attitudes towards immigration have become more relaxed since the EU referendum. Asking the same questions about perceptions of discrimination in 2018, the BES recorded a rise in the extent to which the public perceived discrimination against women (although this rise was mainly seen among women) and ethnic minorities compared to 2016, suggesting that public discussion of such issues permeated the public consciousness. But perceived discrimination against men and white British people remained at similar levels to 2016, suggesting that many white men still believe, in spite of these stories, that they are the ones facing unfair treatment.

FURTHER READING

For more on perceptions of unfair discrimination and disadvantage more broadly, and its consequences for vote choice see, for example, Justin Gest's *The New Minority* (Oxford University Press, 2016) and Ronald Inglehart and Pippa Norris's 'Trump and the Populist Authoritarian Parties: The Silent Revolution in Reverse' (*Perspectives on Politics*, 2017). For the link between perceptions of gendered discrimination and voting in the US see Mark Setzler and Alixandra B. Yanus's 'Why did Women vote for Donald Trump?' (*PS: Political Science & Politics*, 2018). More details on the analysis in this chapter can be found in 'The Gender Backlash in the Vote for Brexit' by Jane Green and Rosalind Shorrocks (Social Science Research Network, 31 July 2019).

CHAPTER 47

Privileged positions? Class and education in the EU referendum

Paula Surridge

In the immediate aftermath of the Brexit vote in 2016, lots of analysis tried to explain what happened by looking at the types of places that voted to Leave or Remain. But this kind of geographical analysis can suffer from what is known as the 'ecological fallacy', where we draw mistaken conclusions about individual behaviour based on how places behave. Just because, say, more working-class areas voted Leave does not necessarily mean that it was working-class people in those areas who were voting to Leave.

Opinion polls published immediately after the vote did not suffer from this problem, but they did have others. They tended to use a crude measure of 'class', and their relatively small size meant that it was not possible to analyse more complex breakdowns of social groups – by age or education, for example. Better-quality data take longer to gather, code and analyse, and while these data are being prepared narratives take on a life of their own and become resistant to new evidence. As a result, claims and counter-claims persist about the extent to which Brexit is (or ever was) the desire of the British working class.

There are in fact two different questions to address about class and voting. The first seeks to explain the character of the Leave and Remain electorates: what proportion, say, of Leave voters are working class? The second focuses on understanding the behaviour of individuals: how likely is it that a member of the working-class voted Leave?

The first question tells us the chances of a Leave voter, selected at random, being drawn from a working-class group. The second tells us the success we would have in guessing the vote of an individual based solely on their class. Both questions are important for understanding the result, but the first question depends to a considerable extent on the relative size of the different groups. This is why, for example, it is common to hear the claim that the Leave vote was largely found in the south or was predominantly middle class – because the majority of the British population (Leave and Remain) are found in these groups.

We must also be clear what we mean by class. Polling companies tend to use a measure of 'social grade', which was designed as a tool for marketing. Academics tend to conceive of social class as an economic category, with classes made up of groups of jobs. Occupational class, as defined by the Office for National Statistics, has eight groups. The largest are the 'lower professional and managerial' and 'intermediate occupations' groups, which together account for around half of the electorate. Those in 'semi-routine' and 'routine occupations', often used as a measure of the 'working class', account for around one in five of the electorate. In the analysis here, professional and managerial occupations are grouped together to form the 'middle class', and those in semi-routine or routine occupations are grouped together to form the 'working class', simplifying this to five groups overall.

Class also overlaps with other social divides that have been shown to be important for voting behaviour. Analyses of the EU referendum vote have consistently shown a strong relationship with education level, particularly whether or not a person has, or is studying for, a degree-level qualification. Education and occupation are, of course, related (though far from perfectly). Some analysts include education as an integral part of social class, but it is better to keep them separate, as they shape political behaviour in different ways.

To disentangle the effects of occupational group and educational qualifications requires good-quality data, with good measures of both class and education and a large sample size. The British Election Internet Panel Study (BEIPS), used here, had a sample size of over 23,000, meaning that even the smallest combination of education and occupation group (which was large employers and higher managerial without degrees) has a decent-sized sample available for analysis.

The figure shows how education and occupational class related to voting in the referendum. Each bar shows the proportion of people with that combination of occupation and education who voted Leave. Reading across the bars of the same shade shows the differences between occupational groups, keeping education level constant. The differences between the bars in each occupational group show the education differences within social classes.

The differences between the bars within occupational groups are much greater than the differences across the occupational groups. For example, the difference between the middle class and working class without degrees is 8 percentage points; for those with degrees, this difference is even smaller, whereas the 'diploma divide' within each is more than 20 percentage points. The class difference is dwarfed by that between those with and those without degrees.

SHARE OF THE VOTE FOR LEAVE BY OCCUPATIONAL CLASS AND EDUCATIONAL LEVEL

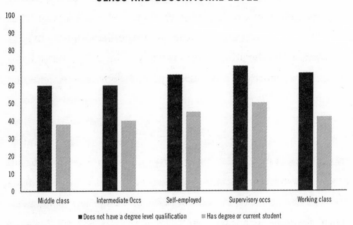

Source: British Election Panel Study, Wave 9 (June/July 2016).

This might be thought to be due to the relationship between age and education level, as higher education has expanded so much over the last two decades. Those with degrees are on average younger than those without a higher education. But a similar analysis replacing occupational class with age group shows the same pattern: among the youngest age group, those without degree-level education were more likely to vote Leave than Remain. This effect is related to the values people hold about the kind of world they would like to live in. Those with degree-level qualifications are far more likely to hold liberal values, such as being against censorship and the death penalty and being more tolerant towards unconventional lifestyles. These same values are closely connected to EU referendum votes, with Remain voters also being considerably more liberal on these issues than Leave voters.

You would therefore be far more successful in guessing a person's vote if you knew whether they held a degree-level qualification than you would be if you knew only their age or their occupational group. Trying to explain the Brexit vote without engaging with education effects is likely to be at best flawed and at worst misleading about causes and consequences of the vote.

FURTHER READING

For more detailed analysis of the referendum see Geoff Evans and Anand Menon's *Brexit and British Politics* (Polity Press, 2017) or Matthew Goodwin and Oliver Heath's 'Brexit vote explained: poverty, low skills and lack of opportunities' (Joseph Rowntree Foundation, 2016). For more on class and British politics more widely see Geoff Evans and James Tilley's *The New Politics of Class* (Oxford University Press, 2017) or Claire Ainsley's *The New Working Class* (Policy Press, 2018). Moving beyond Brexit, *Cultural Backlash* by Pippa Norris and Ronald Inglehart (Cambridge University Press, 2019) explores the link between social values and populism, while the role of education and class in realigning politics across Europe and beyond is explored in Russell Dalton's *Political Realignment* (Oxford University Press, 2018).

—CHAPTER 48—

Did anyone know what they were voting for? Leavers' and Remainers' knowledge of the EU

Lindsay Richards

Ever since the Brexit referendum of 2016, a frequent refrain from Remain campaigners has been that 'they' – by which they mean Leave voters – 'didn't know what they were voting for'. While it may be comforting for losers to believe that the winning side's voters were ignorant and misled, is it true?

To put this assumption to the test, we designed a quiz to compare levels of EU knowledge among Leavers and Remainers, which we put to a sample of voters.

The fifteen questions in the quiz ranged from the easy ('Switzerland is a member state of the EU. True or false?') to the more challenging ('The European Central Bank sets interest rates for the Eurozone. True or false?'), in order to be able to tease apart those with low knowledge from the middling from the real experts.

Contrary to the conventional wisdom among EU supporters, there were no differences overall between the scores of Leavers and

Remainers. Both sides got on average nine out of fifteen items correct. The first half of the table shows a sample of the questions – with the percentages getting them right – and shows how small the differences were. This remains true even when we control for age, education and a host of other things that might relate to political knowledge.

Perhaps the more interesting finding, however, is how ideological differences influence political knowledge. Nine items in the quiz were designed to be 'ideologically neutral'; the remainder were more 'ideologically convenient' for one side or the other.

For example, the case for leaving the EU is perhaps stronger if membership entails an upfront cost for the UK, so believing that 'the UK currently pays more money into the EU than it gets back in the form of subsidies and other funds' is true is more ideologically convenient for Leave voters. Ditto for 'the British government cannot sign free trade deals while Britain is a member of the EU' [true] and 'the EU makes up a larger proportion of the world economy today than it did twenty years ago' [false].

On the other hand, the case for leaving the EU is arguably weaker if the UK's net contribution makes up a relatively small proportion of government spending. So, rejecting the claim that 'more than 10 per cent of British government spending goes to the EU' is more ideologically convenient for Remain voters. The same applies to 'the EU employs more civil servants than the British government' [false] and 'the EU is the world's second largest economy' [true].

Just as predicted, both Leave and Remain voters were more likely to answer questions correctly if the correct responses were ideologically convenient, either due to what is called motivated reasoning (where I pick the answer that best suits my political position) or motivated information seeking (where I only read about the arguments relevant to my side). Despite the vanishingly small differences on the neutral questions, on the three questions designed to be more convenient for Leavers, Leavers were on average 16 percentage points more likely to get the answer right. On the three questions more convenient for Remainers, Remainers were 12 percentage points more likely to get the answer right.

PERCENTAGE GIVING THE CORRECT ANSWER TO THE QUIZ QUESTIONS, BY EU REFERENDUM VOTE CHOICE

	LEAVE VOTERS	REMAIN VOTERS
SAMPLE 'IDEOLOGICALLY NEUTRAL' QUESTION		
Switzerland is a member of the EU [F]	77	74
This is a photograph of Mario Draghi, president of the European Central Bank [T]	68	70
The European Central Bank sets interest rates for the Eurozone [T]	71	71
SAMPLE 'IDEOLOGICALLY-CONVENIENT' FOR LEAVERS QUESTION		
The UK currently pays more money into the EU than it gets back in the form of subsidies and other funds [T]	88	61
SAMPLE 'IDEOLOGICALLY CONVENIENT' FOR REMAINERS QUESTION		
More than ten per cent of British government spending goes to the EU [F]	28	50

Note: Results from five questions that were part of a fifteen-item quiz. Weights applied. N = 3,000. Data collected online in March 2018. Questions are all true/false questions. Correct answers in square brackets.

One (fair) criticism that might be levelled at these findings is that the data come from 2018, two years after the referendum. It is at least plausible that Leavers were less informed in 2016 than Remainers, but – perhaps stung by the criticism from their opponents – have become more knowledgeable since. But this doesn't seem to be the case. Back in 2015, before the referendum, the

Eurobarometer Survey included three simple questions about the EU. When Britons' scores are disaggregated by their image of the EU, there is not much of a difference between those who had a 'very positive image of the EU' and those who had a 'very negative image of the EU' (which is the best proxy available for Leave versus Remain preference). Similarly, a pre-referendum study by Ipsos MORI showed that those intending to vote Leave were more likely to know that the UK paid in more to the EU than it got back, whereas Remainers were more accurate (or, technically, less inaccurate) when it came to the size of the EU's bureaucracy.

There are plenty of differences between Leavers and Remainers, but knowledge of the EU does not appear to be one of them, either before or after the vote. The 2015 data also suggested that the UK had the lowest average scores out of all twenty-eight member states overall. In terms of knowledge, it seems more likely that very few people really knew very much about what they were voting for, regardless of which side they were on, and in a still-divided Britain it might do both sides good to bear in mind that we are all more likely to remember what is convenient and forget what is troublesome.

FURTHER READING

The full results of the study reported here can be found in Noah Carl et al.'s 'Leave and Remain voters' knowledge of the EU after the referendum of 2016' (*Electoral Studies*, 2019). For convincing evidence of the tendencies towards perceptions of fact that fit pre-existing ideological or cultural affinity groups see 'Ideology, motivated reasoning, and cognitive reflection' by Dan Kahan (*Judgment and Decision Making*, 2013). For an easy read about how ill-informed Brits were about the EU see Simon Hix's 'Brits know less about the EU than anyone else' (European Politics and Policy, LSE, 2015).

'Politics is supposed to be the second oldest profession. I have come to realise that it bears a very close resemblance to the first.'

– RONALD REAGAN

—CHAPTER 49—

The real divide: political choice between the sheets

Bernadeta Wilk

Politics divides us more than we realise. A considerable body of research has found cultural differences between conservatives and liberals that extend way beyond their politics: what they eat and drink, what sort of jokes make them laugh, what sort of art and music they like, what sort of cars they drive. One study even showed differences in how tidy their bedrooms are.

And it is not just the tidiness of bedrooms that reveals political divides, but what we do in them. In January 2014, a nationally representative sample of British adults was asked about their own sexual behaviour and fantasies in a YouGov poll. The different demographic profile of each party's supporters means it is necessary to control for the age, gender, marital status and sexual orientation of respondents in order to identify the differences that are genuinely down to political allegiance rather than social background, but even after doing so there was a sharp divide between the parties usually considered of the right and those of the left.

Conservative supporters' bedroom lives were, well, conservative. They were more likely to describe their sexual behaviour as 'consistent' and 'conventional' and less likely to report fantasising about, or taking part in, a wide range of more exotic sexual behaviour. Conservatives were confident about their bedroom prowess, promising more frequent sex than others, and less shyness. Conservative supporters were the only ones to report bedding politicians more than average. They were also more likely than other respondents to report fantasising about sex with a sports star.

Supporters of UKIP, then the new kids on the right-wing block, were if anything even more conventional: they were more likely to describe themselves as lazy, and definitely not 'exciting', in the bedroom; they claimed to avoid sex with younger partners (which, for most UKIP supporters, ruled out a lot of people) and their principal sexual fetish – in fantasy and reality – was the vibrator.

The sexual reports of left-wing partisans, though, were quite different.

Labour partisans had high opinions of themselves in the bedroom: they were more likely to report long-lasting, exciting and varied sex and less likely to report being 'fast'. Labour supporters were also more experimental, in both fantasy and behaviour. They were more likely to report a wide range of fantasies. Some fantasies – such as passionate kissing and sex with a stranger – attracted Labour supporters but repelled Conservative supporters, and there were no fantasies over-reported by both parties' supporters. Labour supporters' sexual behaviour was also more experimental; they were more likely than the average voter to have engaged in threesomes and bondage and to have flings with sports stars, TV stars and older partners, while only MPs turn Tory voters' heads.

Like Labour supporters, Liberal Democrat partisans were often imaginative and experimental in the bedroom. Indeed, an even wider range of sexual behaviours were over-reported by Liberal Democrat backers than Labour partisans, including erotic massage, orgies, sex with someone from a different ethnicity and sex with a trans person. Lib Dem fantasies also tend in exotic directions, featuring bondage, sex on film and watching others.

After the European referendum, we asked the original study sample how they voted. The table below shows the key differences between Leave and Remain voters, again after controlling for age, gender, marital status and sexual orientation. It therefore highlights the behaviour and fantasies which are more frequently, and less frequently, reported by each side's supporters once these things have been controlled for.

Compared to Leave voters, supporters of remaining in the European Union were much more sexually adventurous. They were more likely to fantasise about a range of different sexual behaviours, including sex with someone of the opposite sex, sex with someone of the same sex, sex with someone of a different ethnic background and role-playing. There was only one fantasy Leavers were more likely than Remainers to have: to watch others have sex. You can insert your own joke here.

When it came to reported behaviour – things they claimed to have actually done, rather than thought about – Remainers were also more likely to list a wider range of activities, including having threesomes or sex *al fresco*, filming themselves having sex, or taking part in cross-dressing. By contrast, having sex with a sports star was the only behaviour reported more often by Leave voters than by Remainers. Remainers were also more likely to describe their sex as long-lasting, if infrequent. Again, the jokes write themselves.

BEHAVIOUR AND FANTASIES OF REMAIN AND LEAVE VOTERS

	VOTED REMAIN	VOTED LEAVE
Over-represented self descriptions	Long-lasting, infrequent	Nothing
Over-represented behaviour	Sex with someone of the opposite sex, with a stranger, with a TV or movie star, with a musician, outdoors, a threesome (two men, one woman), passionate kissing, filming yourself having sex, cross-dressing	Sex with a sports star
Over-represented fantasies	Sex with someone of the opposite sex, of the same sex, of different ethnic background, with a work colleague, outdoors, oral sex (giving or receiving), anal sex (giving), role playing, passionate kissing	Watching others having sex

Source: YouGov, 2014–16.

What all this highlights is that the differences which draw people into rival political camps stretch far beyond politics. This isn't to argue that voters are more or less likely to be attracted to the parties as a result of this behaviour – do not expect slogans such as 'Vote Conservative. We're less keen on spanking' – but the differences in values and outlook expressed in politics are also found in many other parts of life, including the bedroom. Voters who prefer a stable and orderly life appear to lean towards conventional sex and conservative politics; those who embrace the new and unconventional may be more attracted to aspects of left-wing politics as well as to sexual experimentation. Political divides don't just reflect narrow differences of opinion about health policy or the deficit; they are also expressions of personality and outlook. Think carefully before talking politics when out on a date: you may be revealing more about yourself than you realise.

FURTHER READING

Predisposed by John R. Hibbing et al. (Routledge, 2014) is an excellent introduction to the field of non-political partisan differences. Of the hundreds of more detailed studies see, for example, Glenn D. Wilson's 'Ideology and Humor Preferences' (*International Political Science Review*, 1990) and his 'Conservatism and Art Preferences' (*Journal of Personality and Social Psychology*, 1973). Tidy bedrooms (and offices) are examined in 'The Secret Lives of Liberals and Conservatives: Personality Profiles, Interaction Styles and the Things They Leave Behind' by Dana R. Carney et al. (*Political Psychology*, 2008). *Why Women Have Better Sex Under Socialism*, by Kristen Ghodsee (Nation Books, 2018), ranges much further than its title suggests.

CHAPTER 50

It's not what it looks like: sex, lies and cheating politicians

Joe Twyman

Sometime in the early 2000s, I appeared on a local radio station to discuss a survey YouGov had carried out into what people thought constituted infidelity.

'So tell us,' the presenter asked, 'what activity is most likely to be counted as cheating?'

'Well, actually it was ana—'

'Thank you. Joe Twyman there from YouGov.'

That was the end of that. They've not invited me back since.

Fast forward a decade and a bit. When, in 2019, Deltapoll (my new company) carried out a similar survey, it discovered that having anal sex with someone who was not your partner was, perhaps to the surprise of very few, still considered by most people to count as cheating (88 per cent said it would always count, along with another 6 per cent who said it would usually be cheating), more so than any of the other seven activities we polled on.

At the other end of the scale came kissing on the cheek, which a mere (but very censorious) 7 per cent think is always cheating.

However they defined it, though, 23 per cent of people admitted that they themselves had cheated on a partner. Even via the anonymity of an online survey, it is worth keeping in mind that data from questions of such a personal nature can suffer from what pollsters call 'social desirability bias' – in other words, people answering in the way they think they should. Still, almost a quarter were happy to admit infidelity, and when we asked how often they had cheated – on a ten-point scale – some 27 per cent of these answered in the upper half of the range. Despite all the differences in sexual behaviour between partisans noted in the previous chapter, here there were relatively few differences between supporters of the different parties or between Leavers and Remainers. Liberal Democrat supporters admitted to cheating a bit more often, but the sample size was for them pretty low. Infidelity, it seems, is one of the few things that can bring our divided nation together.

But what about when politicians cheat, which they do sometimes, apparently. How do we judge them?

Another Deltapoll survey, also in 2019, asked respondents to imagine an MP who had been discovered to have had an affair with someone for over a year while, all that time, keeping it a secret from their partner and family – and then asked them how they felt about this person. Overall, a majority (67 per cent) said they would not be surprised by the news; a plurality (39 per cent) said they would feel less trusting towards the MP in future, although – perhaps because they had such low expectations to begin with – another 34 per cent said it would make no difference; 47 per cent said they would think less highly of the MP; and respondents were fairly evenly divided between whether the MP should resign (34 per cent) or not (36 per cent), with another 30 per cent saying 'Don't know'.

A handful of people gave what seem like curious responses to these questions. Some 9 per cent said that hearing that an MP had had an affair would make them think more highly of them, and the same number said they would trust them more as a result. Maybe they think politicians with flaws are more interesting or authentic, but maybe it is a good reminder that in any survey some people misunderstand the question or give the wrong response by mistake.

A more serious problem with testing things like the way we react to political scandals is that because politicians are – with rare exceptions – party people, their behaviour often gets viewed through partisan filters. When a politician we like or support misbehaves, it can be dismissed as an indiscretion or a mistake. When it is one we do not favour, their behaviour becomes a mortal sin and we call for the scaffold.

To test this, the sample was randomly divided into four groups, with one quarter each asked specifically about a Labour, Conservative, Leave or Remain MP. And it is here that things get a bit more interesting.

For example, shown a Labour MP who had cheated, a plurality of Labour voters (40 per cent) thought that individual should stay in post, compared to 32 per cent who thought they should resign (a net resignation score of -8). But when it was a Conservative MP who was said to have erred, you get the opposite: a plurality of Labour voters thought they should go (a net score of +19).

As the figure below shows, Conservatives are no more consistent. When Conservative-voting respondents were told a Labour MP had cheated, a plurality thought they should resign (+6);

presented with a Conservative MP who had had an affair, a plurality thought they should hang on (-23).

NET SUPPORT FOR RESIGNATION

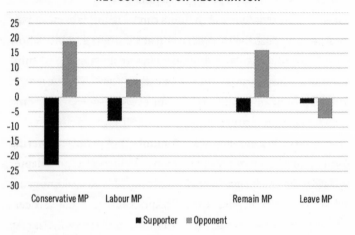

The figures for the Remain/Leave divide, frequently such a strong predictor of attitudes, here produced slightly less clear-cut findings. If the misbehaving MP was a Remainer, Leavers thought they should resign (+16), but if they were told the naughty MP was a Leaver, they narrowly thought they should stay in post (-2).

Remainers were more consistent. Shown a Remainer MP who had had an affair, a plurality of Remainers thought they should stay in office (-5) and they thought the same if the MP was a Leaver (-7). This rare outbreak of consistency may be a sign that Remainers are more socially liberal (which we know from other surveys); it might also at least in part be because Remainers included (almost all) Lib Dem supporters, a group who were less keen on resignation regardless of the identity of the MP. In turn, this might be because Lib Dems were themselves more socially liberal – or it might be because, being aware of the difficulties many Lib Dem MPs have had with matters of the flesh, they are painfully aware that this could mean a lot of by-elections.

Given how strong partisan filters can be in other areas of politics, what is perhaps most striking about these figures is how there is always a non-trivial minority (around a quarter to a third of respondents) who are willing to call for the resignation even of one of their own supporters. Not everyone sees everything through partisan filters.

Plus, there are quite significant numbers of people answering 'Don't know' to all of these questions. As discussed in Chapter 25, it is quite normal in political surveys to find that women are more likely to give 'Don't know' responses – and that was certainly true with this survey. Yet it was not true in the earlier survey about what counted as infidelity. There, it was men who mostly seemed more unsure. Readers should feel free to draw their own conclusions from that.

FURTHER READING

Great Parliamentary Scandals by Matthew Parris (Robson Books, 2004) is now a bit dated but still contains plenty of evidence that politicians do, occasionally, err, and parts of Isabel Hardman's *Why We Get the Wrong Politicians* (Atlantic Books, 2018) are a sombre read on the pressures that life at Westminster can put on politicians' marriages. There's plenty of reading on the problems of social desirability bias in these sorts of surveys, such as 'Measuring sexual behaviour: methodological challenges in survey research' by Kevin A. Fenton et al. (*Sexually Transmitted Infections*, 2001).

Bibliography

Achen, Christopher H. and Bartels, Larry M., *Democracy for Realists: Why Elections Do Not Produce Responsive Government* (Princeton: Princeton University Press, 2016)

Adler, David and Ansell, Ben, 'Housing and Populism', *West European Politics* (2019)

Ainsley, Claire, *The New Working Class: How to Win Hearts, Minds and Votes* (Bristol: Policy Press, 2018)

Almond, Gabriel and Verba, Sidney, *The Civic Culture* (Princeton: Princeton University Press, 1963)

Ansell, Ben W., 'The Politics of Housing', *Annual Review of Political Science* (2019), vol. 22, pp. 165–85

Ariely, Dan, *The (Honest) Truth About Dishonesty: How We Lie to Everyone – Including Ourselves* (London: Harper Collins, 2012)

Arzheimer, Kai and Evans, Jocelyn, 'Geolocation and voting: Candidate–voter distance effects on party choice in the 2010 UK general election in England', *Political Geography* (2012), vol. 31, no. 5, pp. 301–10

Ashcroft, Michael and Culwick, Kevin, *Pay Me Forty Quid and I'll Tell You: The 2015 election campaign through the eyes of the voters* (London: Biteback Publishing, 2015)

Association of Electoral Administrators, 'Elections and Individual Electoral Registration – The Challenge of 2015' [http://www.aea-elections.

co.uk/wp-content/uploads/2015/07/aea-report-elections-and-ier-chal-lenge-of-2015.pdf] (July 2015)

Banducci, Susan; Karp, Jeffrey; Thrasher, Michael and Rallings, Colin, 'Ballot Photographs as Cues in Low-Information Elections', *Political Psychology* (2008), vol. 29, no. 6, pp. 903–17

Bar, Moshe; Neta, Maital and Linz, Heather, 'Very First Impressions', *Emotion* (2006), vol. 6, no. 2, pp. 269–78

Bara, Judith, 'A Question of Trust: Implementing Party Manifestos', *Parliamentary Affairs* (2005), vol. 58, no. 3, pp. 585–99

Bélanger, Éric and Meguid, Bonnie M., 'Issue Salience, Issue Ownership and Issue-Based Vote Choice', *Electoral Studies* (2008), vol. 27, no. 3, pp. 477–91

Bishop, George F., *The Illusion of Public Opinion: Fact and Artifact in American Public Opinion Polls* (Oxford: Rowman & Littlefield, 2005)

Bishop, George F.; Oldendick, Robert W.; Tuchfarber, Alfred J. and Bennett, Stephen E., 'Pseudo-Opinions on Public Affairs', *Public Opinion Quarterly* (1980), vol. 44, no. 2, pp. 198–209

Blinder, Scott; Ford, Robert and Ivarsflaten, Elisabeth, 'The Better Angels of Our Nature: How the Antiprejudice Norm Affects Policy and Party Preferences in Great Britain and Germany', *American Journal of Political Science* (2013), vol. 57, no. 4, pp. 841–57

Bobo, Lawrence, D.; Charles, Camille Z.; Krysan, Maria and Simmons, Alicia D., 'The *Real* Record on Racial Attitudes' in Marsden, Peter V. (ed.), *Social Trends in American Life: Findings from the General Social Survey Since 1972* (Princeton: Princeton University Press, 2012), pp. 38–83

Bochel, J. M. and Denver, D. T., 'Canvassing, Turnout and Party Support: An Experiment', *British Journal of Political Science* (1971), vol. 1, no. 3, pp. 257–69

British Election Study Team, 'Youthquake – a reply to our critics' [https://www.britishelectionstudy.com/bes-impact/youthquake-a-reply-to-our-critics/#.XOQGaC3Myu4] (12 February 2018)

Broughton, David and ten Napel, Hans-Martien (eds), *Religion and Mass Electoral Behaviour in Europe* (London and New York: Routledge, 2000)

Butler, Daniel M. and Broockman, David E., 'Do Politicians Racially Discriminate Against Constituents? A Field Experiment on State Legislators', *American Journal of Political Science* (2011), vol. 55, no. 3, pp. 463–77

Butler, Judith, *Undoing Gender* (New York and London: Routledge, 2004)

Campbell, David E., *Why We Vote: How Schools and Communities Shape Our Civic Life* (Princeton: Princeton University Press, 2006)

Campbell, Rosie, 'What Do We *Really* Know about Women Voters? Gender, Elections and Public Opinion', *Political Quarterly* (2012), vol. 83, no. 4, pp. 703–10

Campbell, Rosie and Cowley, Philip, 'Rich Man, Poor Man, Politician Man: Wealth Effects in a Candidate Biography Survey Experiment', *British Journal of Politics and International Relations* (2014), vol. 16, no. 1, pp. 56–74

— —, 'What Voters Want: Reactions to Candidate Characteristics in a Survey Experiment', *Political Studies* (2014), vol. 62, no. 4, pp. 745–65

Carl, Noah; Richards, Lindsay and Heath, Anthony, 'Leave and Remain voters' knowledge of the EU after the referendum of 2016', *Electoral Studies* (2019), vol. 57, pp. 90–98

Carman, Christopher; Johns, Robert and Mitchell, James, *More Scottish than British? The 2011 Scottish Parliament Election* (Basingstoke: Palgrave Macmillan, 2014)

Carney, Dana R.; Jost, John T.; Gosling, Samuel D. and Potter, Jeff, 'The Secret Lives of Liberals and Conservatives: Personality Profiles, Interaction Styles and the Things They Leave Behind', *Political Psychology* (2008), vol. 29, no. 6, pp. 807–40

Carreras, Miguel; Irepoglu Carreras, Yasemin and Bowler, Shaun, 'Long-Term Economic Distress, Cultural Backlash, and Support for Brexit', *Comparative Political Studies* (2019), OnlineFirst, pp. 1–29

Clarke, Harold D. and McCutcheon, Allan L., 'The Dynamics of Party Identification Reconsidered', *Public Opinion Quarterly* (2009), vol. 73, no. 4, pp. 704–28

Clements, Ben, *Religion and Public Opinion in Britain: Continuity and Change*
(Basingstoke: Palgrave Macmillan, 2015)

Colantone, Italo and Stanig, Piero, 'Global Competition and Brexit', *American Political Science Review* (2018), vol. 112, no. 2, pp. 201–18

Converse, Philip, 'The nature of belief systems in mass publics' in Apter,
David E. (ed.), *Ideology and Discontent* (New York: New York Free Press
of Glencoe, 1964), pp. 47–76

Cowley, Philip and Kavanagh, Dennis, *The British General Election of 2015*
(Basingstoke: Palgrave Macmillan, 2016)

— —, *The British General Election of 2017* (Basingstoke: Palgrave Macmillan, 2018)

Curtice, John, 'One Nation Again', *British Social Attitudes* (1996), vol. 13,
pp. 1–17

— —, 'Why Leave Won the UK's EU Referendum', *Journal of Common Market Studies* (2017), vol. 55, no. S1, pp. 19–37

Curtice, John and Firth, David, 'Exit Polling in a Cold Climate: the BBC–
ITV Experience in 2005 (with discussion)', *Journal of the Royal Statistical
Society Series A* (2008), vol. 171, no. 3, pp. 509–39

Curtice, John; Fisher, Stephen D. and Kuha, Jouni, 'Confounding the Commentators: How the 2010 Exit Poll Got it (More or Less) Right', *Journal
of Elections, Public Opinion and Parties* (2011), vol. 21, no. 2, pp. 211–35

Curtice, John; Fisher, Stephen; Kuha, Jouni and Mellon, Jonathan, 'Surprise,
Surprise! (Again) The 2017 British General Election Exit Poll', *Significance*
(2017), vol. 14, no. 4, pp. 26–9

Curtis, Chris, 'Brexit Basil and Bremain Bridget – How British fictional
characters might vote' [https://yougov.co.uk/topics/politics/articles-re-
ports/2016/05/29/britains-characters-brexit] (29 May 2016)

Cutts, David and Fieldhouse, Edward, 'What Small Spatial Scales Are Relevant as Electoral Contexts for Individual Voters? The Importance of the Household on Turnout at the 2001 General Election', *American Journal of Political Science* (2009), vol. 53, no. 3, pp. 726–39

Dalton, Russell J., *Political Realignment: Economics, Culture, and Electoral Change* (Oxford: Oxford University Press, 2018)

Dennison, James and Goodwin, Matthew, 'Immigration, Issue Ownership and the Rise of UKIP', *Parliamentary Affairs* (2015), vol. 68, no. S1, pp. 168–87

Denver, David and Hands, Gordon, *Modern Constituency Electioneering: Local Campaigning in the 1992 General Election* (London: Frank Cass, 1997)

Dorling, Danny, 'It is necessarily so', *Significance* (2013), vol. 10, no. 2, pp. 37–9

— —, 'Tolerance, inequality and the recession', *Sheffield Political Economy Research Institute Blog*, 1 March 2013

— —, *All That Is Solid: How the Great Housing Disaster Defines Our Times, and What We Can Do About It* (London: Penguin, 2015)

Electoral Commission, 'The December 2015 Electoral Registers in Great Britain: Accuracy and Completeness of the Registers in Great Britain and the Transition to Individual Electoral Registration' [http://www.electoralcommission. org.uk/__data/assets/pdf_file/0005/213377/The-December-2015-electoral-registers-in-Great-Britain-REPORT.pdf] (July 2016)

Erikson, Robert S.; Mackuen, Michael B. and Stimson, James A., *The Macro Polity* (Cambridge: Cambridge University Press, 2002)

Evans, Geoffrey and Mellon, Jonathan, 'Immigration, Euroscepticism, and the rise and fall of UKIP', *Party Politics* (2019), vol. 25, no. 1, pp. 76–87

Evans, Geoffrey and Menon, Anand, *Brexit and British Politics* (Cambridge: Polity Press, 2017)

Evans, Geoffrey and Tilley, James, *The New Politics of Class: The Political Exclusion of the British Working Class* (Oxford: Oxford University Press, 2017)

Evans, Jocelyn; Arzheimer, Kai; Campbell, Rosie and Cowley, Philip, 'Candidate Localness and Voter Choice in the 2015 General Election in England', *Political Geography* (2017), vol. 59, pp. 61–71

Evans, Jocelyn and Tonge, Jonathan, 'Social Class and Party Choice in Northern Ireland's Ethnic Blocs', *West European Politics* (2009), vol. 32, no. 5, pp. 1012–30

Fenton, Kevin A.; Johnson, Anne M.; McManus, Sally and Erens, Bob, 'Measuring sexual behaviour: methodological challenges in survey research', *Sexually Transmitted Infections* (2001), vol. 77, no. 2, pp. 84–92

Fieldhouse, Edward; Green, Jane; Evans Geoffrey; Mellon, Jonathan; Prosser, Christopher; Schmitt, Hermann and van der Eijk, Cees, *Electoral Shocks: The Volatile Voter in a Turbulent World* (Oxford: Oxford University Press, 2019)

Fieldhouse, Edward and Cutts, David, 'The Companion Effect: Household and Local Context and the Turnout of Young People', *Journal of Politics* (2012), vol. 74, no. 3, pp. 856–69

— —, 'Shared Partisanship, Household Norms and Turnout: Testing a Relational Theory of Electoral Participation', *British Journal of Political Science* (2018), vol. 48, no. 3, pp. 807–23

Finifter, Ada W., 'Dimensions of Political Alienation', *American Political Science Review* (1970), vol. 64, no. 2, pp. 389–410

Fisher, Justin; Cutts, David and Fieldhouse, Edward, 'The electoral effectiveness of constituency campaigning in the 2010 British general election: The "triumph" of Labour', *Electoral Studies* (2011), vol. 30, no. 4, pp. 816–28

Fisher, Justin; Cutts, David; Fieldhouse, Edward and Rottweiler, Bettina, 'Constituency Campaigning at the 2015 General Election', paper presented at the Elections, Public Opinion & Parties Specialist Group Conference, Cardiff (2015)

— —, 'The Impact of Electoral Context on the Electoral Effectiveness of

District-Level Campaigning: Popularity Equilibrium and the Case of the 2015 British General Election', *Political Studies* (2018) OnlineFirst, pp. 1–20

Fisher, Stephen D.; Heath, Anthony F.; Sanders, David and Sobolewska, Maria, 'Candidate Ethnicity and Vote Choice in Britain', *British Journal of Political Science* (2015), vol. 45, no. 4, pp. 883–905

Fisher, Stephen D. and Renwick, Alan, 'The UK's referendum on EU membership of June 2016: How expectations of Brexit's impact affected the outcome', *Acta Politica* (2018), vol. 53, no. 4, pp. 590–611

Foos, Florian and de Rooij, Eline, 'All in the Family: Partisan Disagreement and Electoral Mobilization in Intimate Networks—A Spillover Experiment', *American Journal of Political Science* (2017), vol. 61, no. 2, pp. 289–304

Ford, Robert and Goodwin, Matthew, *Revolt on the Right: Explaining Support for the Radical Right in Britain* (London: Routledge, 2014)

Gerber, Alan S.; Green, Donald P. and Larimer, Christopher W., 'Social Pressure and Voter Turnout: Evidence from a Large-scale Field Experiment', *American Political Science Review* (2008), vol. 102, no. 1, pp. 33–48

Gest, Justin, *The New Minority: White Working Class Politics in an Age of Immigration and Inequality* (Oxford: Oxford University Press, 2016)

Ghodsee, Kristen R., *Why Women Have Better Sex Under Socialism: And Other Arguments for Economic Independence* (New York: Nation Books, 2018)

Goodwin, Matthew and Heath, Oliver, 'Brexit vote explained: poverty, low skills and lack of opportunities' [https://www.jrf.org.uk/report/brexit-vote-explained-poverty-low-skills-and-lack-opportunities] (31 August 2016)

— —, 'The 2016 Referendum, Brexit and the Left Behind: An Aggregate-level Analysis of the Result', *Political Quarterly* (2016), vol. 87, no. 3, pp. 323–32

Green, Donald; Palmquist, Bradley and Schickler, Eric, *Partisan Hearts and Minds: Political Parties and the Social Identities of Voters* (New Haven: Yale University Press, 2004)

Green, Jane; Hellwig, Tim and Fieldhouse, Ed, 'Who Gets What: The Group-Based Economic Vote for Brexit' (forthcoming paper)

Green, Jane and Prosser, Chris, 'Women, men, and the 2017 general election' [https://www.britishelectionstudy.com/bes-findings/women-men-and-the-2017-general-election-by-jane-green-and-chris-prosser/] (31 January 2018)

Green, Jane and Shorrocks, Rosalind, 'The Gender Backlash in the Vote for Brexit' (Social Science Research Network, 31 July 2019)

Hanretty, Chris, 'Areal interpolation and the UK's referendum on EU membership', *Journal of Elections, Public Opinion and Parties* (2017), vol. 27, no. 4, pp. 466–83

Hardman, Isabel, *Why We Get the Wrong Politicians* (London: Atlantic Books, 2018)

Heath, Anthony; Fisher, Stephen; Rosenblatt, Gemma; Sanders, David and Sobolewska, Maria, *The Political Integration of Ethnic Minorities in Britain* (Oxford: Oxford University Press, 2013)

Heath, Oliver, 'Policy Representation, Social Representation, and Class Voting in Britain', *British Journal of Political Science* (2015), vol. 45, no. 1, pp. 173–93

Henderson, Ailsa, *Hierarchies of Belonging: National Identity and Political Culture in Scotland and Quebec* (Montreal-Kingston: McGill-Queen's University Press, 2007)

Henderson, Ailsa; Jeffery, Charlie; Wincott, Dan and Wyn Jones, Richard, 'How Brexit was made in England', *British Journal of Politics and International Relations* (2017), vol. 19, no. 4, pp. 631–46

Hibbing John R.; Smith, Kevin B. and Alford, John R., *Predisposed: Liberals, Conservatives, and the Biology of Political Differences* (London: Routledge, 2014)

Hix, Simon, 'Brits know less about the EU than anyone else' [https://blogs.lse.ac.uk/europpblog/2015/11/27/brits-know-less-about-the-eu-than-anyone-else/] (27 November 2015)

Hobolt, Sara B., 'The Brexit vote: a divided nation, a divided continent', *Journal of European Public Policy* (2016), vol. 23, no. 9, pp. 1259–77

Hobolt, Sara B.; Leeper, Thomas J. and Tilley, James, 'Divided by the Vote: Affective Polarization in the Wake of Brexit' [https://s3.us-east-2.amazonaws.com/tjl-sharing/assets/DividedByTheVote.pdf] (2018)

— —, 'Emerging Brexit identities' [https://ukandeu.ac.uk/emerging-brexit-identities/] (3 February 2018)

Holmes, Mary, *What is Gender? Sociological Approaches* (London: Sage, 2007)

Horrie, Chris and Chippindale, Peter, *Stick It Up Your Punter! The Uncut Story of the Sun Newspaper* (London: Heinemann, 1990)

Hudson, David and van Heerde-Hudson, Jennifer, 'A Mile Wide and an Inch Deep', *International Journal of Development Education and Global Learning* (2012), vol. 4, no. 1, pp. 5–23

Inglehart, Ronald and Norris, Pippa, 'The Developmental Theory of the Gender Gap: Women and Men's Voting Behaviour in Global Perspective', *International Political Science Review* (2000), vol. 21, no. 4, pp. 441–63

— —, 'Trump and the Populist Authoritarian Parties: The Silent Revolution in Reverse', *Perspectives on Politics* (2017), vol. 15, no. 2, pp. 443–54

Issenberg, Sasha, *The Victory Lab: The Secret Science of Winning Campaigns* (New York: Broadway Books, 2012)

Iyengar, Shanto and Krupenkin, Masha, 'Partisanship as Social Identity; Implications for the Study of Party Polarization', *The Forum* (2018), vol. 16, no. 1, pp. 23–45

Jacobson, Gary C., 'How Do Campaigns Matter?', *Annual Review of Political Science* (2015), vol. 18, pp. 31–47

Jeffery, Charlie; Wyn Jones, Richard; Henderson, Ailsa; Scully, Roger and Lodge, Guy, 'Taking England Seriously: The New English Politics: The Future of England Survey 2014' [https://www.centreonconstitutionalchange.

ac.uk/sites/default/files/news/Taking%20England%20Seriously_The%20
New%20English%20Politics.pdf] (2014)

Jennings, Will and Stoker, Gerry, 'The Divergent Dynamics of Cities and
Towns: Geographical Polarisation and Brexit', *Political Quarterly* (2019),
vol. 90, no. S2, pp. 155–66

Jennings, Will and Wlezien, Christopher, 'Distinguishing between Most
Important Problems and Issues?', *Public Opinion Quarterly* (2011), vol.
75, no. 3, pp. 545–55

— —, 'Election Polling Errors Across Time and Space', *Nature Human Behaviour* (2018), vol. 2, no. 4, pp. 276–83

Johns, Robert and Shephard, Mark, 'Facing the Voters: The Potential Impact
of Ballot Paper Photographs in British Elections', *Political Studies* (2011),
vol. 59, no. 3, pp. 636–58

Johnston, Ron and Pattie, Charles, *Putting Voters in Their Place: Geography
and Elections in Great Britain* (Oxford: Oxford University Press, 2006)

Johnston, Ron; Pattie, Charles and Rossiter, David, 'A re-dividing nation?
A newly polarised electoral geography of Great Britain', *British Politics*
(2017), vol. 12, no. 4, pp. 521–35

Johnston, Ron; Rossiter, David; Manley, David; Pattie, Charles; Hartman,
Todd and Jones, Kelvyn, 'Coming full circle: The 2017 UK general election and the changing electoral map', *The Geographical Journal* (2018),
vol. 184, no. 1, pp. 100–108

Kahan, Dan M., 'Ideology, Motivated Reasoning, and Cognitive Reflection',
Judgment and Decision Making (2013), vol. 8, no. 4, pp. 407–24

Kahneman, Daniel, *Thinking, Fast and Slow* (London: Allen Lane, 2011)

Katwala, Sunder and Ballinger, Steve, *Mind the Gap: How the Ethnic Minority Vote Cost Theresa May her Majority* (London: British Future, 2017)

Kellner, Peter 'Why Northerners Don't Vote Tory' [http://yougov.co.uk/
news/2013/10/21/why-northerners-dont-vote-tory/] (21 October 2013)

Kennedy, Courtney; Blumenthal, Mark; Clement, Scott; Clinton, Joshua D.; Durand, Claire; Franklin, Charles; McGeeney, Kyley; Miringoff, Lee; Olson, Kristen; Rivers, Douglas; Saad, Lydia; Witt, G. Evans and Wlezien, Christopher, 'An Evaluation of the 2016 Election Polls in the United States', *Public Opinion Quarterly* (2018), vol. 82, no. 1, pp. 1–33

Korris, Matt, 'A Year in the Life: From Member of Public to Member of Parliament' [https://assets.ctfassets.net/rdwvqctnt75b/4ZgkQrromIO4I6y6Qoo WCE/5a186b1ba880d4b5780aee67f03f6564/Publication__A-Year-In-the-Life-From-Member-of-Public-to-Member-of-Parliament.pdf] (June 2011)

Kroh, Martin and Tucci, Ingrid, 'The Party Identification of Germany's Immigrant Population: Parties Should Not Fear Eased Naturalization Requirements', *German Institute for Economic Research* (2010), vol. 6, no. 4, pp. 20–26

LeDuc, Lawrence, 'Referendums and Elections: How Do Campaigns Differ?' in Farrell, David M. and Schmitt-Beck, Rüdiger (eds), *Do Political Campaigns Matter? Campaign Effects in Elections and Referendums* (London: Routledge, 2001), pp. 145–62

Lefevere, Jonas; Tresch, Anke and Walgrave, Stefaan, 'Introduction: Issue Ownership', *West European Politics* (2015), vol. 38, no. 4, pp. 755–60

Lerner, Jennifer S. and Keltner, Dacher, 'Fear, anger, and risk', *Journal of Personality and Social Psychology* (2001), vol. 81, no. 1, pp. 146–59

MacAllister, Ian, 'The dynamics of one-partyism', *Llafur* (1980), vol. 3, no. 2, pp. 79–89

Mac an Ghaill, Máirtín and Haywood, Chris, *Gender, Culture and Society: Contemporary Femininities and Masculinities* (Basingstoke: Palgrave Macmillan, 2007)

McDonald, Michael P. and Popkin, Samuel L., 'The Myth of the Vanishing Voter', *American Political Science Review* (2001), vol. 95, no. 4, pp. 963–74

Marcus, George E.; Neuman, W. Russell and MacKuen, Michael B., *Affective intelligence and political judgment* (Chicago: University of Chicago Press, 2000)

Marsh, David; O'Toole, Theresa and Jones, Su, *Young People and Politics in the UK: Apathy or Alienation?* (Basingstoke: Palgrave Macmillan, 2007)

Martin, Nicole S., 'Ethnic minority voters in the UK 2015 general election: A breakthrough for the Conservative party?', *Electoral Studies* (2019), vol. 57, pp. 174–85

Martin, Nicole and Khan, Omar, 'Ethnic Minorities at the 2017 British General Election' [https://www.runnymedetrust.org/uploads/2017%20Election%20 Briefing.pdf] (February 2019)

Martin, Nicole; Sobolewska, Maria and Begum, Neema, 'Left Out of the Left Behind: Ethnic Minority Support for Brexit' (Social Science Research Network, 2019)

Mattes, Kyle and Milazzo, Caitlin, 'Pretty Faces, Marginal Races: Predicting Election Outcomes using Positive and Negative Trait Assessments of British Parliamentary Candidate Images', *Electoral Studies* (2014), vol. 34, pp. 177–89

Mattinson, Deborah, *Talking to a Brick Wall: How New Labour Stopped Listening to the Voter and Why We Need a New Politics* (London: Biteback Publishing, 2010)

Mellon, Jonathan; Evans, Geoffrey; Fieldhouse, Edward; Green, Jane and Prosser, Christopher, 'Aggregate Turnout Is Mismeasured' [http://dx.doi. org/10.2139/ssrn.3098436] (8 January 2018)

— —, 'Brexit or Corbyn? Campaign and Inter-Election Vote Switching in the 2017 UK General Election', *Parliamentary Affairs* (2018), vol. 71, no. 4, pp. 719–37

Mellon, Jonathan; Prosser, Christopher; Urban, Jordan and Feldman, Adam, 'Which Promises Actually Matter? Understanding Promissory Representation with Conjoint Analysis of Election Pledges' [http://dx.doi.org/10.2139/ ssrn.3283813] (13 November 2018)

Mitchell, David, *Politics and peace in Northern Ireland: Political parties and the implementation of the 1998 Agreement* (Manchester: Manchester University Press, 2015)

Moon, Nick, *Opinion Polls: History, Theory and Practice* (Manchester: Manchester University Press, 1999)

MRS, 'MRS Guidance Note on Collecting Data on Sex and Gender' [https://www.mrs.org.uk/pdf/Guidance%20on%20Collecting%20Data%20on%20Sex%20and%20Gender.pdf] (January 2016)

Naurin, Elin, *Election Promises, Party Behaviour and Voter Perceptions* (Basingstoke: Palgrave Macmillan, 2011)

Newport, Frank, 'In U.S., 87% Approve of Black-White Marriage, vs. 4% in 1958' [https://news.gallup.com/poll/163697/approve-marriage-blacks-whites.aspx] (25 July 2013)

Nickerson, David W., 'Is Voting Contagious? Evidence from Two Field Experiments', *American Political Science Review* (2008), vol. 102, no. 1, pp. 49–57

Norris, Pippa and Inglehart, Ronald, *Sacred and Secular: Religion and Politics Worldwide* (Cambridge: Cambridge University Press, 2004)

— —, *Cultural Backlash: Trump, Brexit, and Authoritarian Populism* (Cambridge: Cambridge University Press, 2019)

O'Grady, Tom, 'Careerists Versus Coal-Miners: Welfare Reforms and the Substantive Representation of Social Groups in the British Labour Party', *Comparative Political Studies* (2019), vol. 52, no. 4, pp. 544–78

O'Leary, Brendan, *A Treatise on Northern Ireland, Volume III: Consociation and Confederation* (Oxford University Press, 2019)

Olson, Ingrid R. and Marshuetz, Christy, 'Facial Attractiveness is Appraised in a Glance', *Emotion* (2005), vol. 5, no. 4, pp. 498–502

Palan, Kay M.; Areni, Charles S. and Kiecker, Pamela, 'Re-examining Masculinity, Femininity, and Gender Identity Scales', *Marketing Letters* (1999), vol. 10, no. 4, pp. 363–77

Panagopoulos, Costas; Larimer, Christopher W. and Condon, Meghan, 'Social Pressure, Descriptive Norms, and Voter Mobilization', *Political Behavior* (2014), vol. 36, no. 2, pp. 451–69

Parris, Matthew and Maguire, Kevin, *Great Parliamentary Scandals: Five Centuries of Calumny, Smear and Innuendo* (London: Robson Books, 2004)

Patel, Tina G. and Connelly, Laura, '"Post-race" racisms in the narratives of "Brexit" voters', *The Sociological Review* (2019), OnlineFirst, pp. 1–17

Pinker, Steven, *The Better Angels of Our Nature: A History of Violence and Humanity* (London: Penguin, 2012)

Prosser, Chris; Fieldhouse, Ed; Green, Jane; Mellon, Jonathan and Evans, Geoff, 'The myth of the 2017 youthquake election' [https://www.britishelectionstudy.com/bes-impact/the-myth-of-the-2017-youthquake-election/#.XOQF7i3Myu4] (29 January 2018)

Rallings, Colin; Thrasher, Michael and Borisyuk, Galina, 'Unused votes in English Local Government Elections: Effects and Explanations', *Journal of Elections, Public Opinion and Parties* (2009), vol. 19, no. 1, pp. 1–23

de Rooij, Eline; Green, Donald P. and Gerber, Alan S., 'Field Experiments on Political Behavior and Collective Action', *Annual Review of Political Science* (2009), vol. 12, pp. 389–95

Rosenbaum, Martin, 'Local voting figures shed new light on EU referendum' [https://www.bbc.co.uk/news/uk-politics-38762034] (6 February 2017)

Särlvik, Bo and Crewe, Ivor, *Decade of Dealignment: The Conservative Victory of 1979 and Electoral Trends in the 1970s* (Cambridge: Cambridge University Press, 1983)

Schuman, Howard and Presser, Stanley, 'Public Opinion and Public Ignorance: The Fine Line between Attitudes and Nonattitudes', *American Journal of Sociology* (1980), vol. 85, no. 5, pp. 1214–25

— —, *Questions and Answers in Attitude Surveys: Experiments of Question Form, Wording, and Context*, reprint edn (London: Sage, 1996)

Scotto, Thomas J.; Reifler, Jason; Hudson, David and van Heerde-Hudson, Jennifer, 'We Spend How Much? Misperceptions, Innumeracy, and Support for the Foreign Aid in the United States and Great Britain', *Journal of Experimental Political Science* (2017), vol. 4, no. 2, pp. 119–28

Setzler, Mark and Yanus, Alixandra B., 'Why Did Women Vote for Donald Trump?', *PS: Political Science & Politics* (2018), vol. 51, no. 3, pp. 523–7

Shorrocks, Rosalind, 'Modernisation and government socialisation: Considering explanations for gender differences in cohort trends in British voting behaviour', *Electoral Studies* (2016), vol. 42, pp. 237–48

Sides, John and Vavreck, Lynn, *The Gamble: Choice and Chance in the 2012 Presidential Election* (Princeton: Princeton University Press, 2014)

Sloam, James and Henn, Matt, *Youthquake 2017: The Rise of Young Cosmopolitans in Britain* (Basingstoke: Palgrave Macmillan, 2019)

Smith, Matthew, 'How British fictional characters might vote: 2017 general election edition' [https://yougov.co.uk/topics/politics/articles-reports/2017/06/06/how-british-fictional-characters-might-vote-2017-g] (6 June 2017)

— —, 'Margaret Thatcher: the public view 40 years on' [https://yougov.co.uk/topics/politics/articles-reports/2019/05/03/margaret-thatcher-public-view-40-years] (3 May 2019)

Sobolewska, Maria, 'Is Labour losing the ethnic minority vote?', *New Statesman* (5 January 2015)

Stockemer, Daniel, 'Electoral Participation: How to Measure Voter Turnout?', *Social Indicators Research* (2017), vol. 133, no. 3, pp. 943–62

Sturgis, Patrick; Baker, Nick; Callegaro, Mario; Fisher, Stephen; Green, Jane; Jennings, Will; Kuha, Jouni; Lauderdale, Ben and Smith, Patten, *Report of the Inquiry into the 2015 British general election opinion polls* (London: Market Research Society and British Polling Council, 2016)

Sturgis, Patrick and Jennings, Will, 'Why 2017 may have witnessed a Youthquake after all', LSE British Politics and Policy Blog, 6 December 2018

Sturgis, Patrick and Smith, Patten, 'Fictitious Issues Revisited: Political Inter-est, Knowledge and the Generation of Nonattitudes', *Political Studies* (2010), vol. 58, no. 1, pp. 66–84

Swift, Art, 'Americans' Worries About Race Relations at Record High' [https://news.gallup.com/poll/206057/americans-worry-race-relations-re-cord-high.aspx] (15 March 2017)

Tesler, Michael, 'The Spillover of Racialization into Evaluations of Bo Obama' [http://today.yougov.com/news/2012/04/10/spillover-racialization-evalu-ations-bo-obama/] (10 April 2012)

— —, *Post-Racial or Most-Racial?: Race and Politics in the Obama Era* (Chi-cago: University of Chicago Press, 2016)

Thomson, Robert; Royed, Terry; Naurin, Elin; Artés, Joaquín; Costello, Rory; Ennser-Jedenastik, Laurenz; Ferguson, Mark; Kostadinova, Petia; Moury, Catherine; Pétry, François and Praprotnik, Katrin, 'The Fulfill-ment of Parties' Election Pledges: A Comparative Study on the Impact of Power Sharing', *American Journal of Political Science* (2017), vol. 61, no. 3, pp. 527–42

Thrasher, Michael; Borisyuk, Galina; Rallings, Colin and Webber, Rich-ard, 'Candidate Ethnic Origins and Voter Preferences: Examining Name Discrimination in Local Elections in Britain', *British Journal of Political Science* (2017), vol. 47, no. 2, pp. 413–35

Tilley, James, 'We Don't Do God? Religion and Party Choice in Britain', *Brit-ish Journal of Political Science* (2015), vol. 45, no. 4, pp. 907–27

Tilley, James and Hobolt, Sara, 'Is the Government to Blame? An Experi-mental Test of How Partisanship Shapes Perceptions of Performance and Responsibility', *Journal of Politics* (2011), vol. 73, no. 2, pp. 316–30

Todorov, Alexander; Mandisodza, Anesu N.; Goren, Amir and Hall, Crystal C., 'Inferences of Competence from Faces Predict Election Outcomes', *Science* (2005), vol. 308, no. 5728, pp. 1623–6

Tonge, Jonathan and Evans, Jocelyn, 'Northern Ireland: Unionism Loses More Leaders' in Geddes, Andrew and Tonge, Jonathan (eds), *Britain Votes 2010* (Oxford: Oxford University Press, 2010), pp. 158–75

— —, 'Northern Ireland: Another Communal Headcount' in Geddes, Andrew and Tonge, Jonathan (eds), *Britain Votes 2015* (Oxford: Oxford University Press, 2015), pp. 117–32

— —, 'Northern Ireland: Double Triumph for the Democratic Unionist Party' in Tonge, Jonathan; Leston-Bandeira, Cristina and Wilks-Heeg, Stuart (eds), *Britain Votes 2017* (Oxford: Oxford University Press, 2018), pp. 139–54

Vasilopoulou, Sofia and Wagner, Markus, 'Fear, anger and enthusiasm about the European Union: Effects of emotional reactions on public preferences towards European integration', *European Union Politics* (2017), vol. 18, no. 3, pp. 382–405

Wagner, Markus, 'Fear and anger in Great Britain: Blame Assignment and Emotional Reactions to the Financial Crisis', *Political Behavior* (2014), vol. 36, no. 3, pp. 683–703

Wald, Kenneth, *Crosses on the Ballot: Patterns of British Voter Alignment Since 1885* (Princeton: Princeton University Press, 1983)

Webber, Richard; Rallings, Colin; Borisyuk, Galina and Thrasher, Michael, 'Ballot Order Positional Effects in British Local Elections, 1973–2011', *Parliamentary Affairs* (2014), vol. 67, no. 1, pp. 119–36

Westwood, Sean; Messing, Solomon and Lelkes, Yphtach, 'Projecting Confidence: How the Probabilistic Horse Race Confuses and Demobilizes the Public' [https://ssrn.com/abstract=3117054 or http://dx.doi.org/10.2139/ssrn.3117054] (2 February 2019)

Whiteley, Paul; Clarke, Harold; Sanders, David and Stewart, Marianne, *Affluence, Austerity and Electoral Change in Britain* (Cambridge: Cambridge University Press, 2013)

Wilson, Glenn D., 'Ideology and Humor Preferences', *International Political Science Review* (1990), vol. 11, no. 4, pp. 461–72

— —, 'Conservatism and Art Preferences', *Journal of Personality and Social Psychology* (1973), vol. 25, no. 2, pp. 286–8

Wlezien, Christopher, 'The Public as Thermostat: Dynamics of Preferences for Spending', *American Journal of Political Science* (1995), vol. 39, no. 4, pp. 981–1000

Wyn Jones, Richard and Scully, Roger, *Wales Says Yes: Devolution and the 2011 Welsh Referendum* (Cardiff: University of Wales Press, 2012)

Wyn Jones, Richard; Scully, Roger and Trystan, Dafydd, 'Why do the Conservatives always do (even) worse in Wales?', *British Elections and Parties Review* (2002), vol. 12, no. 1, pp. 229–45

Zogby, John, *The Way We'll Be: The Zogby Report on the Transformation of the American Dream* (New York: Random House, 2008)

Zuckerman, Alan; Dasovic, Josip and Fitzgerald, Jennifer, *Partisan Families: The Social Logic of Bounded Partisanship in Germany and Britain* (Cambridge: Cambridge University Press, 2007)

Index

Hof, Dennis 228

house prices 271–5

household voting 183–7

Humphrey the cat 93–5

immigration

and the European Union 247–
51, 255–6

issue ownership on 58–60

Independent, The 19

Intergenerational Foundation 130

Ipsos MORI 103, 172, 249, 251

issue ownership 57–61

Jennings, Will 9

Johnson, Boris xiii

Kennedy, Courtney 111

Labour Party 4

in 2005 general election 70, 108

in 2010 general election 217–18

in 2015 general election 37, 69

in 2017 general election 130–32

class of voters 160–61, 162

class of MPs in 159–61

ethnic minority MPs in 117–18

and ethnic minority voters 154,
171–6

and European referendum 242

and gender voting patterns
149–50

issue ownership 58, 59

localness of candidates 223

and regional voting 189, 191–3

religion of voters 166, 167, 169

and Scottish political culture 197

sexual behaviours of supporters 296–7

and swing voters 140

target voters for 45–6, 47, 48

and voting intentions 21

in Wales 204, 206–7

and youth vote 130–32

Lammy, David 130

Larry the cat 95

Liberal Democrats

in 2010 general election 70–71,
217, 218

in 2015 general election 37–8

localness of candidates 223

sexual behaviours of supporters 297

and voting intentions 21

Liberal Party

religion of voters 166–7

in Wales 203–4

Life and Times 211

polls *cont.*

as replacement for politics xx

rules for understanding xv–xx

scepticism of xiii–xiv, xv

'top-of-the-head' answers in

3–4, 13–17

unusual results in xv–xvi

wording of xiv–xv, xvii

postal voting 229–30

Presser, Stanley 14

public opinion

difficulty in measuring 1–6

nonattitudes in 13–17

on overseas aid 25–9

rationality of 31–5

responsiveness to policy

changes 34–5

and voting intentions 19–23

Pulzer, Peter 171

Reagan, Ronald 293

referendums

public opinion changes 53

regional voting 189–93

religion 165–9

reversion point reversal 54

Roberts, Wyn 205–6

Sanders, Bernie 47

Scottish Election Study 201

Scottish independence referendum

(2014) 53

Scottish National Party (SNP) 143,

166, 189, 197

Schuman, Howard 14

Scotland

constituency campaigning

215–19

independence referendum 53

political culture in 197–202

and regional voting 189, 191

religion in 166, 167, 168, 190–91

swing voters in 143

sexual behaviours 295–9, 301–5

Sinn Féin 209–10, 211, 213

swing voters 139–43

target voters 45–9

Thatcher, Margaret 93–5, 262–3

'top-of-the-head' answers 3–4,

13–17

Trump, Donald xiv

accuracy of polls 7–8

and cultural backlash 279–80

dead voters 228

and economic resentments 268

emotions towards 106

Twyman, Tony xv–xvi